P9-BJH-265

A MANUAL OF SAIL TRIM

Books by Stuart H. Walker

THE TECHNIQUES OF SMALL BOAT RACING (ed.)
THE TACTICS OF SMALL BOAT RACING
PERFORMANCE ADVANCES IN SMALL BOAT RACING (ed.)
WIND AND STRATEGY
ADVANCED RACING TACTICS
WINNING: THE PSYCHOLOGY OF COMPETITION
A MANUAL OF SAIL TRIM

A
MANUAL
OF
SAIL TRIM

by

STUART H. WALKER

Illustrated by

THOMAS C. PRICE

W. W. Norton & Company

New York   London

Copyright © 1985 by Stuart H. Walker
All rights reserved.

Published simultaneously in Canada by Penguin Books Canada Ltd,
2801 John Street, Markham, Ontario L3R 1B4
Printed in the United States of America.

The text of this book is composed in Times Roman, with display
type set in Optima. Composition by Com Com
Manufacturing by Haddon Craftsmen
Book design by Jacques Chazaud

Library of Congress Cataloging in Publication Data

Walker, Stuart H.
A manual of sail trim.

1. Sailboat racing. I. Title.
GV826.5.W285 1985   797.1'24   85-301
ISBN 0-393-03296-5 (soft)

W. W. Norton & Company, Inc., 500 Fifth Avenue,
New York, N.Y. 10110
W. W. Norton & Company Ltd., 37 Great Russell Street,
London WC1B 3NU

4 5 6 7 8 9 0

Contents

Foreword   *7*

1. Principles of Sail Trim   *11*

2. The Fractional Rig   *31*

3. Sail Controls   *39*
   Upwind   39
   Reaching   73
   Running   86

4. Crew Movement Techniques   *97*

5. Gears   *105*
   Go Gear (Acceleration)   105
   Low Leeway Gear   107
   Pointing Gear   109
   Starting Gear   112

6. Special Conditions: Upwind   *116*
   Yawing Balance   116
   Dirty Air   118
   Waves   122
   Gust Control   129
   Light Air   132
   Moderate Air   138
   Heavy Air   142
   Very Heavy Air   146

7. Special Conditions: Reaching   *149*
   Light and Moderate Air Reaching   149

Heavy Air Reaching   156

8. Special Conditions: Running   *163*
    Light and Moderate Air Running   163
    Heavy Air Running   170

9. Maneuvers   *179*
    Tacking   179
    Reach-to-Reach Jibe   183
    Running Jibe   189
    Spinnaker Hoist   192
    Spinnaker Drop   194
    Spinnaker Set While Jibing   199
    Bearing Away   202
    Luffing   204
    Passing on the Reach   206
    Blanketing   211

10. Organization   *215*
    The Trim Chart   215
    Control Systems   219
    Control Methods   229

Glossary   *237*

Charts   *243*
    Chart 1. Summary: Gears and Controls   244
    Chart 2. Sail Selection Chart   245
    Chart 3A. Blank Trim Chart   246
    Chart 3B. Light Air Mainsail and Jib   248
    Chart 3C. Heavy Air Mainsail and Jib   250

Foreword

When writing the foreword to my last book, I indicated that psychology might be the most important determinant of outcome in sailboat racing. I am tempted to change my mind, to announce now that speed is the most important, that with speed little else matters. But I believe I can have it both ways! With speed, tactics are simplified, strategy need only be conservative. Therefore, with speed, one's psyche is at ease; the relaxed, confident attitude that generates success results. With speed, the only way one can lose is because one's psyche requires it. Thus, psychology remains the most important determinant of outcome, but speed is the most important determinant of psychology! "Nothing makes a helmsman look (and feel) better than a fast boat!"

And, of course, it is sail trim that determines boat speed. Anytime you hear differently, wonder whether the speaker is gullible, naive, or trying to set you up. Smooth bottoms, weight, windage, etc., are of little significance—except to believers.

Tony Marchaj has said that racing sailboats, even when managed by experts, rarely function at better than 85 percent of their potential V_{mg} (speed made good to windward) and that this failure is due to the "additional drag" associated with inappropriate sail trim. He believes, in fact, that correct trim when it does occur is achieved but momentarily and then by chance. The implication is clear: sail trim produces the significant variations in boat speed and improvement in sail trim provides the big gains in performance.

The manual is intended for use by and will be of value to all racing sailors in all racing sailboats. The size and configuration of the sails involved make relatively little difference. Whether the sail is a genoa jib on an ocean racer or a short-footed jib on a Star, the principles discussed apply. Where differences in application exist, they have been noted in the text.

Most of the principles discussed—particularly those which relate to special circumstances (gust response, waves, dirty air, etc.)—are applicable to all rigs. But the effects of some sail controls on some special rigs (masthead or unstayed, for instance) are sufficiently different that the recommendations made herein are not necessarily applicable.

The concise format is arranged in outline form to provide ready access to needed information and is intended for use prior to, during, and after racing. An understanding of the purpose, action, and application of each sail and rig control is provided and is followed by a thorough presentation of how these controls should be used to achieve optimal performance—to windward, while reaching and running, and during a variety of wind and racing conditions. Special consideration is given to "shifting gears" to achieve different sailing purposes, to managing complex conditions such as dirty air, waves, gusts, light air, etc., and to maneuvers such as tacking, jibing, setting and lowering the spinnaker, and rounding marks.

In this book the racing sailor will have for the first time a reference which will prepare him to establish the optimal sail trim for a particular condition, permit him to reevaluate the extent to which his trim is correct while racing, and allow him to critique his trim retrospectively after a particular event.

The material presented is derived from extensive and continued experience in some of the world's most competitive fleets. The principles presented and the recommendations given have been proved to be applicable in dinghies as well as racing keelboats. Even the most experienced racing sailor will find information herein which is new and which has previously been inadequately understood. Most will find for the first time a resource which fully answers all of their questions about sail trim.

A MANUAL OF SAIL TRIM

1
Principles of Sail Trim

PURPOSE

To supply the energy which, while creating the least possible resistance, will move the hull through the water at the maximum possible speed and, to windward, at the closest possible angle to the wind and at the least possible leeway angle.

PRIMARY CONCERNS

Speed
Pointing
Hydrodynamic Force
Balance
Leeway

POTENTIAL PERFORMANCE

AERODYNAMIC AND HYDRODYNAMIC FORCES

Sails are positioned by sail trim so as to deviate and accelerate the airflow around their leeward surfaces. From this deviation optimal sail trim generates the greatest possible lift (force perpendicular to the airflow) with, to windward, the least possible drag (force in the direction of the airflow) *(Fig. 1.1)*.

Lift (or pressure) is generated because (according to Bernoulli's theorem) the total energy of an airflow cannot change but can be redistributed complementarily between velocity, pressure, and eddy formation. As air deviates around convex leeward surfaces the velocity of its flow increases, and as air attempts to "circulate" in reverse around concave windward surfaces the velocity of its flow decreases *(Fig. 1.2)*. On leeward surfaces, where the velocity increases, lateral

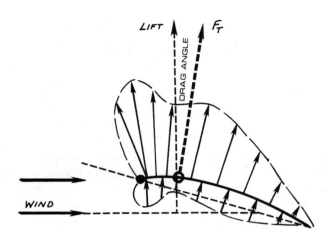

1.1. Aerodynamic forces. The relationship between lift, acting perpendicular to the wind flow, and F_T, the aerodynamic force.

1.2. Deviation of the airflow. Note that the airflow may be viewed as a combination of a circular flow (induced by the sails and the mainsail leech vortex) and the free-stream flow. Note that the flow is accelerated on the leeward surfaces (particularly of the jib) and decelerated on the windward surfaces (particularly of the jib and in the slot) and that the jib is operating in a lift, airflow deviated aft by the main.

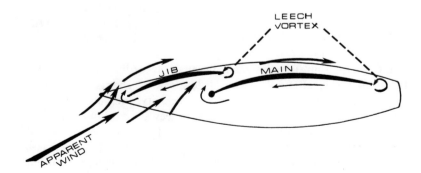

pressure decreases; on windward surfaces, where the velocity decreases, lateral pressure increases. The result is a major "negative" pressure (suction) on leeward surfaces (to the extent that flow is "attached" along them) acting to leeward and a modest positive pressure on windward surfaces acting to leeward. The net pressure acting to leeward, perpendicular to the airflow, is lift; the energy dissipated in eddy formation is drag (a portion of the total resistance).

The effect of the lift and drag forces can be represented as a vector resolving the two, always operating aft of the direction of lift. This resultant aerodynamic force can then be resolved into two components: a driving force acting forward (in the direction headed) and a heeling or side force acting laterally. The driving force causes the boat to move forward and is opposed (at a steady speed) by an equal resistance force acting aft.

A jib (a sail placed ahead, and to leeward, of another) increases the total lift generated by a sail plan of fixed area and makes that sail plan more efficient at typical sailing speeds. Cat rigged boats are more efficient at higher speeds on all points of sailing (C-class catamarans) and are more efficient to windward if the total sail area is small (Lasers, Finns).

The aerodynamic lift and the resultant driving force from a jib are approximately twice as great as from a mainsail of similar area because (1) the leech of a jib is in the zone of accelerated flow to leeward of the mainsail, and the flow over its leeward surface is therefore accelerated by the main; (2) the jib is operating in a lift, in air deviated aft (ahead of and in the "slot") by the main, and therefore its lift is directed more forward; (3) the jib has no mast to disturb the airflow coming on to its leeward surface *(Fig. 1.2)*.

The aerodynamic force produced by a main is less than that of a jib but it is more efficient. The flow over much of its leeward surface (in the "slot") is actually slowed and the pressure differential between its windward and leeward surfaces is diminished. However, the flow off its leech modified by the flow off the leeward surface of the jib induces less drag (less eddying). The net reduction in drag increases the efficiency of the rig as a whole, causes the aerodynamic force to act more forward, and therefore particularly benefits pointing.

The jib-headed sail plan may be considered to operate as a power producing unit forward; the jib, whose design, condition, and trim are the most important determinants of speed; and an efficiency determining unit aft, the mainsail leech, whose design, condition, and trim are almost as important as determinants of pointing, leeway, and balance.

Acceleration occurs when the lift resulting from the deviation of the airflow is transmitted to the hull. Transmission is accomplished because the leading edges of the sails are attached to the mast or the jibstay and their clews are (or should be) attached directly to the hull. Holding a sheet in the hand without the intervention of a winch or ratchet block risks dissipation of the force in movement of one's arm. As the hull, its fins, and the sails move through the water and the air, resistance (due to friction, wave-making, eddy production, etc.) to that movement develops. Acceleration continues until the resistance acting aft equals the driving force acting forward.

When first exposed to the wind, the hull moves to leeward. As it does so, water moves around its fins, and is deviated by them, flowing more rapidly over their windward sides. This deviation creates a hydrodynamic lift force acting perpendicular to the water flow. Because water is so much denser than air, a total hydrodynamic force $(R_T$, see Glossary at end of book) sufficient to equilibrate the total aerodynamic force (F_T) is produced by fins moving at a mere 4–6

1.3. Hydrodynamic forces. The relationship between the wind, the boat speed, and the hydrodynamic force created by waterflow over the fins.

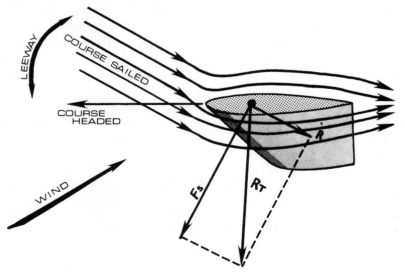

knots and at an angle of incidence of but 3°–5°. When a sufficient hydrodynamic force is created, the hull will move forward and to leeward at its "leeway angle" (3°–5° to its heading) at a steady rate.

All forces, created initially by airflow, whether they tend to cause the boat to move ahead, to slip to leeward, to heel, to pitch, or to turn (or yaw), must be balanced by equal and opposite hydrodynamic forces or static pressures (righting forces, for instance). Whenever these forces are momentarily unbalanced, acceleration—to increase or decrease speed, make more or less leeway, heel, pitch, or yaw—in one direction or another will occur.

Aerodynamic force is primary and supplies all the energy—inadequate, ideally matched to the boat's design, or excessive. The hydrodynamic force, on the other hand, is consequent to the aerodynamic force, due to the movement of the hull through the water *(Fig. 1.3)*. Hydrodynamic force is limited by the limitation on hull speed (approximately 1.3 times the square root of waterline length, except for catamarans, etc.) and the fixed sizes and shapes of the underwater fins. The rudder is the only means by which the hydrodynamic force may be modified. The sails must transmit an aerodynamic force to the hull which can be balanced by the hydrodynamic force available and will not require an inappropriate angulation of the rudder.

Forward motion in the desired direction and at the desired speed results when sail trim (1) causes the amount, direction, and distribution of the available aerodynamic force to match the limited hydrodynamic force (created by the forward motion) and (2) produces a forward-acting, driving force (a component of the total aerodynamic force) sufficient to match the total resistance produced by the forward motion.

SPEED

Power (Driving Force)

DETERMINANTS

Planform

An elliptical (bent top mast, wide upper sail section) planform produces the least induced drag (as the air is then deflected with the same induced velocity all along the trailing edge). The usual triangular sail is a particularly poor planform as it results in a higher induced drag and therefore a lower driving force.

Area

The greater the sail area the greater the aerodynamic force, the greater the side force, and the greater the driving force produced. In order to decrease aerodynamic side force (and the resultant heeling and leeway), sail area can be reduced by either reefing the main or changing to a smaller jib.

Angle of Incidence

The angle of incidence is the most important adjustable determinant of driving force *(Fig. 1.4)*. An increase in the angle of incidence (a low heading angle and/or a narrow sheeting angle) up to the

1.4. Angle of incidence. The relationship of the angle of incidence to the flow over the sails as indicated by the telltales.

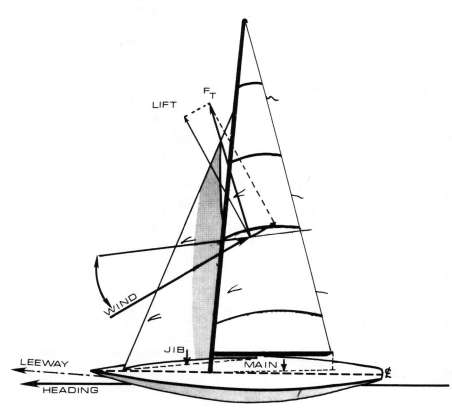

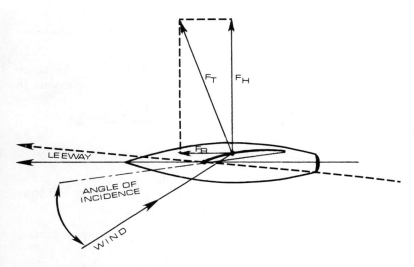

1.5. Angle of incidence. The relationship between the wind, the angle of incidence, and the forces produced by deviating the airflow.

stalling angle increases the driving force at the expense of a relatively greater increase in the side force. The factors determining the angle of incidence are *(Fig. 1.5):*

> Heading angle—heading of the boat relative to the wind
> Sheeting angle—position of the boom or jib lead relative to the centerline of the boat
> Twist—position of the leech relative to the boom or jib lead

The angle of incidence (together with the draft and the position of maximum draft) determines to what extent the airflow will be deviated by a sail (and this determines the lift or aerodynamic force produced by the sail). Deviation and lift are greatest when flow around the leeward surface is attached (occasionally laminar, usually turbulent) and negligible when it is separated (breakaway, stalled) *(Fig. 1.6).* Ordinarily, only the leading edge (the first few feet astern of the luff) of a sail generates laminar flow. Most of the leeward surface has turbulent flow, but only a small area near the leech is stalled. Greater portions of the leeward surface have turbulent flow and are subject to stalling when the angle of incidence is greater or inconstant, the draft is lesser, the position of maximum draft is farther aft, or the airflow is lighter or more erratic.

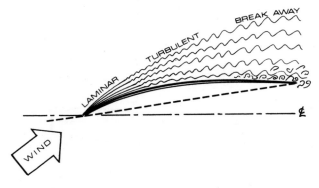

1.6. Attached flow. Attached flow on the forward part of the sail, separation on the after part.

Draft (Fullness) of Sails

The draft of a sail is the next (following the angle of incidence) most important determinant of total aerodynamic force produced—in general, the greater the draft the greater the total force. However, the greater the draft the greater the proportion of side force to driving force and therefore the less efficient the sail to windward. Draft depends upon *(Fig. 1.7):*

Designed draft
Sheet/vang tension—position of leech relative to luff
Foot tension—outhaul or jib sheet tension
Mast bend—fore and aft and lateral
Jibstay sag—fore and aft and lateral
Twist

Position of Maximum Draft

The position of maximum draft modifies the position of the center of effort and, therefore, the yawing moment, the gust response, the ability to point, and the ability of the leading edge to initiate attached leeward surface flow. Draft forward (a full leading edge) facilitates the initiation of attached flow and, therefore, is appropriate to waves, to dirty air, and to gust response. Draft aft (a flat leading edge) is appropriate to pointing in smooth water. The position of maximum draft depends upon:

Designed position of draft
Sheet/vang tension
Luff tension—Cunningham or jib halyard/jib tack downhaul
    tension
Mast bend—fore and aft and lateral
Jibstay sag—fore and aft and lateral

Practical Limitations

INSTABILITY

Sails and fins generate optimal lift at their optimal angle of
incidence.
Whenever the sails and fins are not at their optimal angle of
incidence, they are generating less than optimal lift.
Rolling, pitching, and yawing alter the angle of incidence—the
greater the roll, the pitch, or the yaw (the greater the instability), the greater the stalling, eddying, and vortex formation
(the greater the induced drag) and the lesser the generated lift.

Stability can be improved by:

Minimizing the pitching, rolling, and yawing moments

Reduction in these moments can be achieved by:

Altering the period of free oscillation
Sailing at a different angle or angle of heel
Altering sail trim (particularly the upper sections)

1.7. Sail trim. The elements of sail trim which modify the aerodynamic and
driving forces.

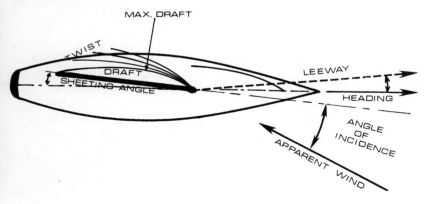

DISTURBED AIR

Wind Shear

The wind velocity (less impeded by surface friction) increases with height above the surface of the water. Therefore, the apparent wind is shifted aft in proportion to height. In addition, the sectional chords of triangular sails decrease with height. The tendency to stalling (separation of flow) is inversely proportional to chord length. Therefore, in order to maintain a consistent angle of incidence and to diminish the risk of stalling, all sails in all conditions must be twisted with height. To the extent that the airflow is irregular (dirty air) and/or the rig is oscillating (pitching, rolling, yawing), the twist must be increased.

Unstable Airflow (Gusts and Lulls)

Unstable airflow alters the angle of incidence and speed and therefore decreases both sail and fin efficiency, induces excess drag, and requires excess rudder use.

Dirty Air (From Other Boats, Etc.)

This decreases sail and fin efficiency and induces excess drag.

LACK OF ADAPTABILITY

Despite every effort to maintain stability, the sail plan is in constant motion (proportionate to the amount of wave action) and is exposed to continuous variation in the strength and direction of the airflow (proportionate to the irregularity of that flow—meteorological turbulence, disturbed air, wind shear, etc.). The sail plan must be made as adaptable as possible to these variations by the following techniques:

Trim Responsiveness

Rapid adjustment in sail trim:
   Main traveler
   Main sheet
   Jib sheet
   Cunningham
   Jib luff

Heading Responsiveness

Rapid variation in heading

Hull Trim Variation

Rapid redistribution of crew weight

Twist

Variation in sheeting angle throughout the height of the sail (always permits some portion of the sail to be at the correct angle of incidence)

Flexibility

Automatic adjustment of the sails to irregular airflows and to movements of the rig associated with yawing, rolling, and pitching:
Flexible mast
Jibstay sag
Control of boom with vang (permits boom to rise and ease leech in gust)

Resistance

Acceleration occurs whenever the aerodynamic force temporarily exceeds the resistance, and deceleration whenever the opposite occurs. The increased speed results in increased eddying, friction, and wave-making. When the altered resistance matches the altered driving force, speed becomes constant once again *(Fig. 1.8)*.

The elements of resistance are:

Sail drag:
Induced drag
Profile drag
Additional drag
Wave-making resistance
Skin friction
Windage
Fin drag

Sail trim, even when it is appropriate, is associated with induced drag (eddies at the edges of the sails) and profile drag (friction at the surface of the sails and the rig) and, when it is inappropriate, with additional drag. Sail trim also affects wave-making resistance (heeling

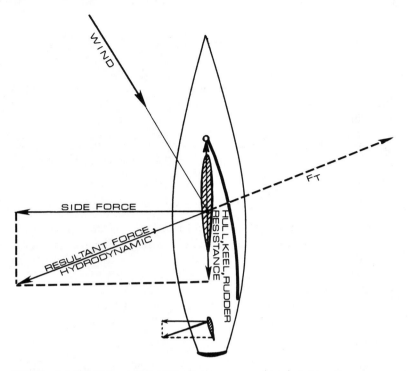

1.8. Resistance. The relationship between speed and resistance.

and instability cause an increase, for instance) and fin drag (imbalance requiring rudder angulation causes an increase, for instance).

INDUCED DRAG

Induced drag is increased by heeling, by instability, and by disturbed air. Whenever the angle of incidence is other than optimal, induced drag (lack of sail efficiency) increases.

ADDITIONAL DRAG

Additional drag is due to the inappropriateness of trim and may be reduced by constant modification of trim and by a rig whose flexibility permits some automatic adaptation to the irregularities of the airflow. (However, the best possible sail trim is probably associated with a failure to attain better than 85 percent of optimal performance. When sail trim is correct, it is only momentarily so and probably by chance rather than design.)

WAVE-MAKING RESISTANCE

Wave-making resistance is increased by heeling, by assuming a large leeway (yaw) angle, by an attitude differing from the designed waterline plane, and by instability.

Due to wave-making, resistance increases exponentially as "hull speed" is approached. Only by rising onto its own bow wave (planing) or by surfing on preexisting waves can this resistance and limitation on speed be overcome.

FIN DRAG

Fin drag is increased by alterations in sailing attitude and by instability (as is wave-making resistance). Whenever the rudder is used to steer the boat (not merely to provide hydrodynamic lift), fin drag is increased. To the extent possible, the boat should be steered by altering sail trim or crew distribution.

POINTING

Pointing is the heading selected, between luffing and stalling, which the helmsman believes to be the most effective in gaining distance to windward, most likely to produce the best V_{mg}.

Gain to windward depends upon speed—because speed determines hydrodynamic lift, and the greater the lift for a given wind velocity the lesser the required leeway angle (the less the leeway)—and upon pointing (heading angle). High pointing depends upon the tolerance of the leading edge of the jib to being aimed high into the wind flow and upon the degree to which all the leeches can be brought up to a position parallel to the course sailed, at the leeway angle (slightly above the centerline), without stalling. When the leading edge splits the wind flow and the leeches are closed to this degree, the greatest possible deviation of the wind flow and the least drag angle (the angle between the lift force, perpendicular to the airflow, and the total aerodynamic force, F_T) result.

Determinants

In moderate air and smooth water when high pointing is appropriate, pointing depends upon the following.

JIB ENTRY FULLNESS

When sailing to windward, the jib luff edge should split the wind flow. To the extent that the entry portion (the foot or so of sail immediately aft of the luff), is flat, the jib (and the boat) can be aimed higher into the wind without luffing. However, the jib will then be less able to establish attached leeward surface flow at any but the optimal angle of incidence and will require exact steering.

The position of maximum draft does not necessarily determine the jib entry fullness but may contribute to it; that is, if the position of maximum draft is aft of mid-chord the jib entry is usually flatter.

LEECH POSITION

When the leeches of both the main and the jib are brought parallel to the leeway angle (above the centerline), the angle of incidence is maximal and the lift force is directed as far aft as possible. This position of the jib leech (parallel to the leeward fullness of the main) causes the flow on the jib's leeward surface to be maximally accelerated and the flow off the jib's leech reduces the induced drag of the main to the minimum. The result is that the sail plan reaches maximal efficiency—with the least induced drag for the lift created and therefore the greatest possible driving force for the aerodynamic side force produced.

At the same time, these leech positions produce the maximum aft deviation of the airflow ahead of the main, to windward of the jib. This means that the jib is operating in the maximum possible lift—that the jib entry can be aimed higher into the wind than with any other conformation and that the jib's leeward surface faces as much forward as possible, maximally improving its efficiency (at that heading angle).

Leech position depends upon sheeting angle (lead or traveler car position), upon heading angle, and upon twist (sheet tension).

Practical Limitations

Waves, which cause instability, and disturbed air, which directly alters the angle of incidence and the lift generated, affect pointing even more than speed. The increased resistance (due to wave-making and fin drag), which characterizes sailing in waves, and the increased induced and additional drag, which characterize sailing in both waves and disturbed air, require that pointing be sacrificed so as to increase driving force (increase sheeting angle and decrease heading angle).

Pointing is also inappropriate in light air, when, because speed and hydrodynamic side force are low, leeway is high and when, because the low-speed airflow attaches with difficulty, the angle of incidence must be low.

HYDRODYNAMIC FORCE

Movement in the desired direction depends upon the creation of a hydrodynamic force which is (1) equal in strength to, (2) in the same direction as, and (3) aligned with (i.e., not offset from) the aerodynamic force *(Fig. 1.9)*.

Strength of the Hydrodynamic Force

The strength of the hydrodynamic force is dependent upon and modified only by the speed of the boat and the leeway angle. If the

1.9. Alignment. The alignment of aerodynamic and hydrodynamic forces to achieve yawing balance.

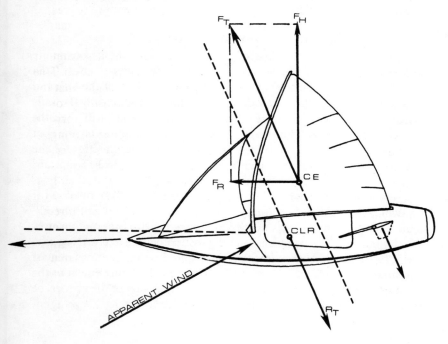

aerodynamic force increases, it must be balanced by an increase in boat speed or by an increase in leeway angle. In light to moderate air an increase in aerodynamic force will produce a significant increase in speed and in the strength of the hydrodynamic force. In heavy air, when speed cannot be significantly increased, hydrodynamic force can only be increased by an increase in leeway angle.

Direction of the Hydrodynamic Force

The direction of the hydrodynamic force is dependent upon the relationship between speed and leeway angle: the greater the speed the more wave-making resistance (hydrodynamic drag) increases, and the more aft the hydrodynamic force is directed; the greater the leeway angle (up to the point of stalling), the more forward (perpendicular to the course) the hydrodynamic force is directed. If the aerodynamic force is directed more forward, if the boat is headed up or the sheeting angle is increased, the boat must (and will) increase speed and direct the hydrodynamic force more aft. If the aerodynamic force is directed more aft (more perpendicular to the course), if the boat is headed off or the sheeting angle is decreased, the leeway angle must (and will) increase and direct the hydrodynamic force more forward.

Alignment of the Hydrodynamic Force

The alignment of the hydrodynamic force with the aerodynamic force depends upon the relative positions of the center of effort (CE) of the sails and the center of lateral resistance (CLR) of the hull and its fins. The boat should be designed so that the CE, with the sails displaced to leeward of the centerline (as they will be), will align the aerodynamic force produced in moderate air (or whatever air the boat is designed to sail in) with the CLR and with the direction of the hydrodynamic force produced by the boat speed typical of that air. In all other winds the two forces will be mal-aligned; that is, their lines of action will be separated by a distance or arm "a." A turning (or yawing) moment will then result (the force, usually taken to be F_H, the laterally acting component of F_a, times the distance "a") which, if the boat is to be kept on course, must be counteracted. Negation of a yawing moment requires that the CE, through alterations in mast position or sail trim (or both), or the CLR, through movement of the centerboard or rudder or through altered angulation of the rudder, be shifted and the arm "a" eliminated.

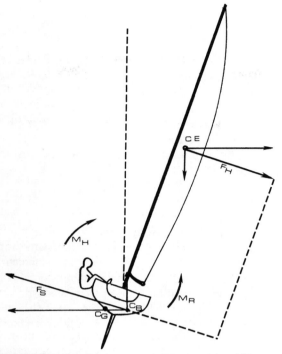

1.10. Heeling forces. Heeling moment and righting moment.

BALANCE IN HORIZONTAL, LATERAL, AND VERTICAL PLANES

Any force which tends to cause the boat to move other than straight forward, upright, and in the plane of her designed waterline increases resistance (wave-making and fin drag, particularly) and leeway.

Balance in the Horizontal Plane (between the strength, direction, and alignments of the hydrodynamic force and the aerodynamic side force)

Depends chiefly upon wind velocity, heeling, sheeting angles, mast position, keel or centerboard and rudder position, rake, relative power (side force) derived from each sail, and position of maximum draft in each sail.

Balance in the Lateral Plane (between the strength, direction, and alignments of the heeling force and the righting force) *(Fig. 1.10)*

Depends chiefly upon wind velocity, angle of incidence and draft (fullness) of the sails, and the righting forces (crew weight, keel weight, etc.) available.

Balance in the Vertical Plane (between the strength, direction, and alignments of the forces of buoyancy and gravity)

Depends chiefly upon mast, keel, gear, and crew position; weight; and weight distribution.

LEEWAY

In order to generate the hydrodynamic lift necessary to counteract the side force produced by the sails when sailing to windward, the hull and its fins must be moved through the water at a sufficient speed and an appropriate angle of incidence. The greater the angle of incidence (leeway angle) short of stalling, the greater the hydrodynamic lift produced for a given speed. The lower the speed the greater is the leeway angle required to produce the necessary hydrodynamic lift. A high leeway angle is therefore characteristic of light air when, although the aerodynamic side force is low, boat speed is low and is characteristic of heavy air when the aerodynamic side force is high and the boat speed, though high, cannot be further increased. Sail trim directly affects leeway because it determines both speed and the aerodynamic side force that must be counteracted.

Determinants

Boat speed
Planform of the fins
Area of the fins
Angle of incidence of the fins
Draft (sectional shape) of the fins
Position of maximum draft of the fins

The only determinant which can be affected by sail trim is boat speed but boat speed is by far the most significant determinant. Even a flat plate fin can be made to generate hydrodynamic lift at a low leeway angle, if speed is sufficiently great. The reciprocal relationship between speed and leeway angle causes speed to be the most important determinant of gain to windward (V_{mg}) in all conditions except moderate air with smooth water. In all other conditions leeway offsets pointing and leeway (the required leeway angle) can only be diminished through an increase in speed.

Practical Limitations

Waves, which cause instability, and imbalance, which causes the boat to move through the water at other than its designed attitude (heeled, yawed, or pitched), alter the angle of incidence of the fins so as to diminish their efficiency, thereby requiring a greater leeway angle for the speed available.

UNMODIFIABLE DETERMINANTS OF PERFORMANCE

WIND VELOCITY

Variation in wind velocity is the major factor necessitating variation in sail trim.

LIGHT AIR

Stage I

Beginning Driving Force, Absent Hydrodynamic Side Force
Apparent wind velocity: 0–2 knots
Primary concerns: power, leeway, and balance

Stage II

Maximum Driving Force Sought but Unattainable
Apparent wind velocity: 2–4 knots
Primary concerns: power and pointing

MODERATE AIR

Stage III

Maximum Heeling Force without Heeling
Apparent wind velocity: 4–8 knots
Primary concerns: pointing and power (insufficient)

Stage IV

Maximum Heeling Force with Moderate, Controlled Heeling
Apparent wind velocity: 8–10 knots
Primary concerns: power and pointing

Stage V
Additional Driving Force at a Fixed Angle of Heel
Apparent wind velocity: 10–14 knots
  Primary concerns: power and heeling (excessive) and pointing

HEAVY AIR

Stage VI
Maximum Driving Force and Boat Speed to Windward
Apparent wind velocity: 14–16 knots
  Primary concerns: power and heeling (excessive) and balance

Stage VII
Maximum Driving Force at a Fixed Angle of Heel
Apparent wind velocity: 16–30 knots
  Primary concerns: leeway, balance, and adaptability

Stage VIII
Decreasing Boat Speed and Marked Leeway
Apparent wind velocity: 30+ knots
  Primary concerns: speed, leeway, and balance

WAVES, GUSTS, DIRTY AIR

Marked variations in the angle of incidence and the velocity of the airflow associated with waves or with irregular airflow (inherent instability or dirty air) necessitate additional alterations in sail trim (superimposed upon the trim appropriate to the wind velocity).

2
The Fractional Rig

EFFECT

The fractional rig provides optimal control of the degree and distribution of mast bend. Control of bend (fore and aft and lateral) and the distribution of bend provide control of mainsail draft and its distribution and, through the effect of mast bend on jibstay sag, permit control of jib draft and its distribution. The fractional rig permits optimal adaptation to a particular main or jib and optimal control of main and jib shape to adapt them to a wide range of wind and wave conditions.

Mast bend, because it alters the position of the mast tip, directly affects main leech tension and, because it alters the position of the jibstay attachment, directly affects jibstay tension.

CONTROL OF MAST BEND

INCREASED MAST BEND (associated with decreased leech tension and increased jibstay sag) *(Fig. 2.1)*

Mast Flexibility

Increased Righting Moment (keel weight, hiking power, etc., transmitted through windward shrouds)

Permanent Backstay Tension (decreased jibstay sag initially, at least, if mast is stiff)

"Pre-Bend" (Positive) *(Fig. 2.2)*

Chocking or pulling or ramming the mast forward at deck level or aft at the step (for a keel-stepped mast)

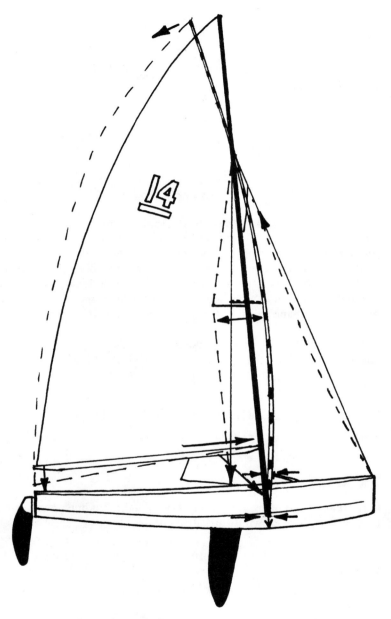

2.1. Fractional rig (without backstays). Note the distribution of tension and the resulting compressive mast bend on a rig without backstays.

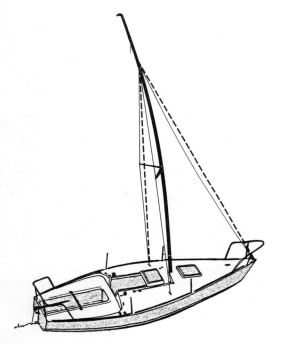

2.2. "Positive" pre-bend. Note means of inducing fore and aft mast bend while decreasing jibstay tension (jibstay sag).

Shroud/spreader relationships which push the mid-mast forward
Spreaders fixed with a deflection greater than the shrouds
Spreaders longer than the mast-shroud distance
Shrouds attached to the deck forward of alignment with fixed
    spreader tips
High shroud tension

Baby Stay Tension

INCREASED MAST BEND—MIXED EFFECTS

Vang Tension

With flexible mid-mast: opens leech and increases jibstay sag (by
    pushing lower mast forward and to windward)
With stiff mid-mast: closes leech and increases jibstay sag (by
    pulling boom down more than it bends lower mast)

DECREASED MAST BEND (associated with increased leech tension and decreased jibstay sag)

Mast Stiffness

Decreased Righting Moment

Decreased Permanent Backstay Tension

"Pre-bend" (Negative) *(Fig. 2.3)*

> Chocking or pulling or ramming the mast aft at deck level or forward at the step (for a keel-stepped mast)
> Shroud-spreader relationships which push the mid-mast aft
> Spreaders fixed with a deflection less than that of the shrouds

2.3. "Negative" pre-bend. Note means of diminishing fore and aft mast bend and increasing jibstay tension with backstay or mainsheet tension (jibstay straight).

Spreaders shorter than the mast-shroud distance
Shrouds attached to the deck aft of alignment with fixed spreader
  tips
Low shroud tension

Jumper Stays (or diamond stays or upper shrouds, if attached
spreaders are swept forward)

Running Backstays (or lower shrouds led aft)

Strut Forward to Deck Affixed at Gooseneck Level

Persisting Tension in Leeward Shroud

If the windward shroud stretches and/or the mid-mast bends
  forward and/or laterally (see causes of Increased Mast Bend),
  the leeward shroud will become slack. The hounds will then
  no longer be fixed but will rotate forward, to windward and
  downward, increasing lower mast bend and jibstay sag.
Vang tension and a stiff topmast increase the slackening of the
  leeward shroud.
Negative "pre-bend" decreases the slackening of the leeward
  shroud.

CONTROL OF THE DISTRIBUTION OF MAST BEND (Fig. 2.4)

Increased Stiffness in One Segment

Increases the bend in the remainder and visa versa, i.e., a flexible
topmast decreases low mast bend.

Local Alterations in Mast Stiffness

Tapering
Altering wall thickness
Cutting away the sail slot
Insertion of an interior stiffener or application of an exterior
  stiffener

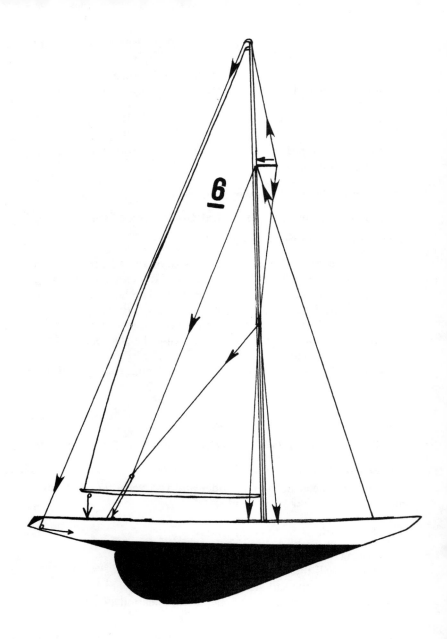

2.4. Fractional rig (with backstays). Note the distribution of tension and the resulting straight mast on a rig with backstays.

DETERMINANTS OF LOCALIZED BEND

Low Bend

Restriction of bend aloft
Vang tension
Strut forward of the mast at the gooseneck
Mainsheet tension—depending upon where the mainsheet is attached to the boom relative to the directly overhead site

Mid-bend

Restriction of bend aloft
Restriction of bend below (at the partner and step)
Shroud attachment site relative to the jibstay attachment
Running backstay tension
Jumper stay tension
Trapeze wire attachment site relative to the shroud attachment site
Baby stay tension

Upper Bend

Restriction of bend below
Permanent backstay tension
Site of attachment of the backstay on the masthead crane

BASIC SETTINGS FOR STANDING RIGGING

Set the jibstay length to provide desired rake.
Optimal rake to windward is (for most boats) the maximum possible. Limitations are as follows.

Mainsail leech length: rake must permit adequate leech tensioning without "two-blocking" the mainsheet.
Jib clew position: rake must permit adequate leech tensioning and an adequate trim angle by the jib sheet.

Set the upper shrouds to maximum tension that does not induce compressive lateral bend in the mast. This keeps the leeward shroud taut to maximum possible wind velocity.

Set the spreader length, spreader angle, and site of attachment of the shrouds to the deck relative to the spreader tips (and/or such devices as mast rams, pullers, and struts) to achieve the desired positive or negative "pre-bend."

Set the lower shrouds (if any) to permit or limit the desired amount of lateral mast bend.

Set backstays (permanent or running), jumper stays, baby stays, etc., to achieve the amount and distribution of fore and aft bend appropriate to the mainsail luff curve.

3

Sail Controls

UPWIND

RAKE (JIBSTAY LENGTH)

Effect

Alters center of effort as well as efficiency of sails to windward; beneficially shifts the centers of maximum draft to a more vertical locus and alters the beneficial "end plate effect" (approximation of the boom and jib foot to the deck); decreases leech tension (unless compensated) of both main and jib *(Fig. 3.1)*.

3.1. Rake. Note the shift of the centers of effort and the change in the relationship of the foot of the jib and the boom to the deck.

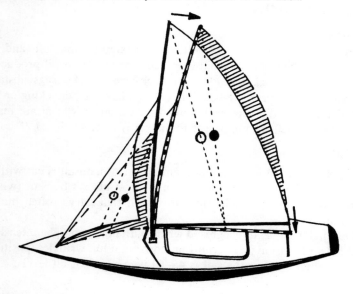

Initial Setting

Set to permit mainsail to be sheeted properly (upper leech approximately parallel to boom) with mast bent appropriately in 10–12 knots of true wind and boom end as low as feasible. To windward "the more rake the better" as both sails become more efficient, rig becomes more flexible (jibstay tension less limiting) and jib head separates from mainsail.

Adjustment

No adjustment is necessary in many boats; adjustments confuse jib lead, mainsheet, etc., settings.

Increase in rake for light air will keep boom down but advantage is slight.

Decrease in rake for heavy air may be necessary to reduce weather yawing moment (and restore balance) and to permit adequate main leech tensioning (i.e., to reduce excessive twist). Twist is usually desirable above 12 knots in waves but in smooth water a decrease in rake and a tighter leech may be faster.

To windward the more rake the better—but downwind the mast must be brought forward of vertical.

MAST BEND (FORE AND AFT)

Effect

Flattens mainsail, moves position of maximum draft aft, and, if produced by backstay or mainsheet, tensions jibstay; or, if produced by vang, swept-back spreaders, or deck-level chocks, sags jibstay; decreases side force. "Pre-bend" may be achieved by chocking or by modifying shroud/swept-back spreader relationships to attain mast bend independent of jibstay (or jib halyard) tension *(Fig. 3.2)*.

Initial Setting

Set for designed luff curve of mainsail; each mainsail is cut with a specific amount of luff round; the mast must always be bent (when sailing to windward) sufficiently to match that curve (often more, never less).

Optimal mast bend recognized when, with no Cunningham tension and halyard tension just permitting horizontal luff wrinkles, position of maximum draft in the sail is 45–50 percent aft at all levels.

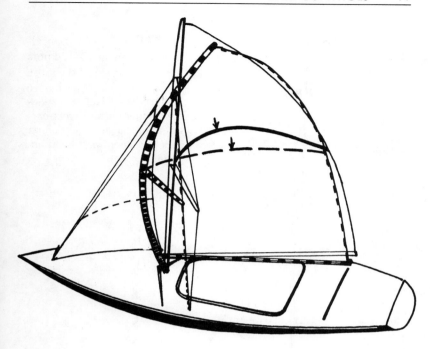

3.2. Mast bend. Note the changes in jib and mainsail fullness and the positions of maximum draft.

Pre-Bend

Pre-bend is useful because it segregates mast bend from jibstay sag. Mast bend sufficient to match the mainsail luff curve may be obtained by chocking (pulling or pushing) the mast at its step or partner with a decrease in jibstay (or jib halyard) tension and by shroud/spreader relationships without excessively tensing the jibstay (or jib halyard) *(Fig. 3.3)*. Such pre-bend is useful in both very light and very heavy air and as a means of preventing inversion while heavy air running. Pre-bend should be limited by innate mast stiffness or a forward strut or running backstays or it will result in excessive bend in moderate air.

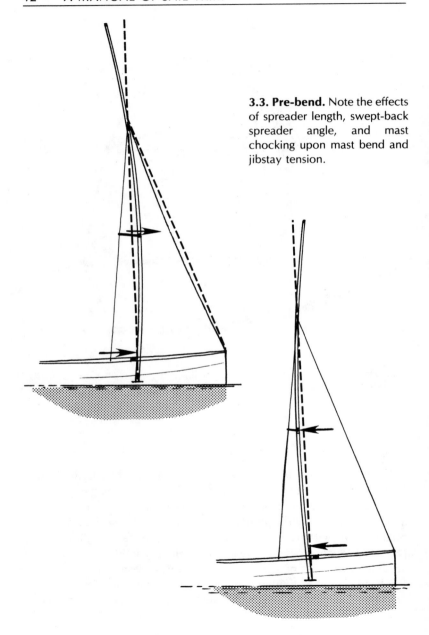

3.3. Pre-bend. Note the effects of spreader length, swept-back spreader angle, and mast chocking upon mast bend and jibstay tension.

Adjustment

Mast bend just matching mainsail luff round is appropriate for optimal boat speed conditions—smooth water (wind speed of 4–14 knots)—and for sailing in waves (wind speed of 4–18 knots).

More mast bend is appropriate for all other conditions—particularly very light and very heavy air—when leeway is excessive. However, the mast should never be bent beyond the degree tolerated by the sail.

Mast bend is the major adjustment for changes in wind velocity alone, that is, without associated changes in wave size: the flatter the sea the more mast bend increment for a given change in wind velocity; the lumpier the sea the less mast bend increment (and the more twist) for a given change.

Mast bend in most dinghies is responsive—to wind strength and to gusts—and may be sufficient to the requirement. In racing keelboats, sufficient mast bend must be deliberately contrived (by backstay tension, vang tension, mast chocking, shroud tension, etc.). Optimal backstay tension is indicated by the position of maximum draft in the upper third of the mainsail—usually 50 percent aft of the luff.

Backstay tension modifies jibstay sag directly and, though it should be used primarily to set mainsail shape, should be coordinated with pre-bend, lateral mast bend, and vang tension to assure that it does not adversely affect jibstay sag.

MAST BEND (LATERAL)

Effect

Alters fullness and position of maximum draft of mainsail and thus the aerodynamic force (power) produced. If the upper mast section falls to leeward, the lower section will open to windward (proportionate to the stiffness of the upper mast). The upper sail is flattened and the power is reduced. If the lower mast section sags to leeward, the lower sail is made fuller, draft moves aft, and power is increased. Side force and heeling force decrease if the masthead falls off, and vice versa *(Fig. 3.4)*.

On many boats lateral mast bend is the most readily available technique to achieve optimal mainsail luff curvature without an excessive increase in jibstay tension. It may be used (with or without

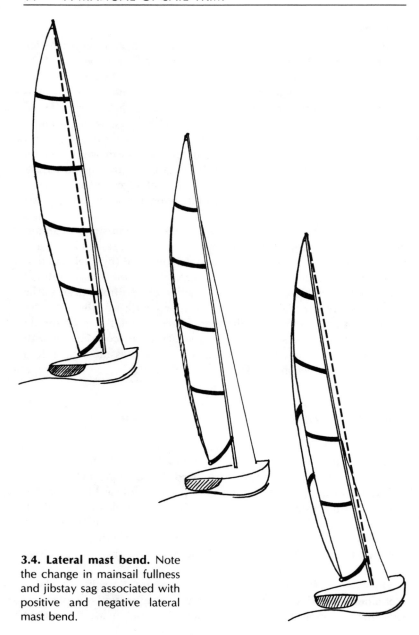

3.4. Lateral mast bend. Note the change in mainsail fullness and jibstay sag associated with positive and negative lateral mast bend.

"pre-bend") to limit the effects of shroud, backstay, and mainsheet tension on jibstay sag. Negative lateral mast bend (sag) increases jibstay sag and mainsail fullness; fore and aft bend (except "pre-bend") decreases jibstay sag and mainsail fullness.

Initial Setting

Set shrouds so that mast stands straight laterally (in 8–14 knots depending upon the sail, the sheeting angle used, and the righting moment available) when maximum righting moment (with full sails) is just capable of keeping boat at the optimal angle of heel; this setting will result in the masthead falling to leeward in stronger winds and, depending upon the rig, may permit the mast below the hounds to sag to leeward in light winds. Optimal lateral mast control should keep the mast straight through static shroud loading in light air, permit negative bend (sag to leeward) due to sail loading in moderate air, re-straighten the mast as the boom and the mainsail leech pull the mast tip to leeward in strong air, and allow the lower mast to bend to windward (separating the main from the jib) as the vang attached to the offset boom drives the lower mast to windward in very heavy air. In a dinghy appropriate pressures and limitations on a flexible mast will cause this to happen automatically; in a keel boat it will have to be induced.

The site of attachment of the upper shrouds and/or of the trapeze wire will affect lateral mast bend, attachment above the jibstay preventing mast tip falloff and lower mast bend to windward (but facilitating pre-bend).

Adjustments

MODERATE AIR

Adjust shrouds or spreaders so that the mast below the hounds sags to leeward. Mainsail will become fuller and draft will move aft thereby creating an appropriate mainsail shape for moderate air without using other techniques (backstay, mainsheet, etc.) which would increase jibstay tension.

HEAVY AIR

Adjust shrouds so that masthead falls to leeward (particularly if needed to compensate for a full mainsail or a lightweight crew).

Mainsail will become flatter and draft will move forward, thereby countering the tendency in strong winds for the sail to become fuller and its draft to move aft; heeling force will be reduced aloft; and the mainsail will separate from the jib (a means of reducing the mainsail's induced drag).

Relation to Backstay, Mainsheet, and Jibstay Tension

If the sails in use are incompatible with one another in a particular sailing condition, the resultant inappropriate jibstay sag can be modified by altering lateral mast bend. Sagging the mid-mast to leeward increases jibstay sag and makes the mainsail fuller; permitting the upper mast to fall to leeward also increases jibstay sag but makes the mainsail flatter. The backstay and mainsheet can be set to achieve the required jibstay sag and then the lateral mast bend can be modified to attain the desired mainsail shape, or the lateral mast bend can be set to attain the required mainsail shape and then the backstay and mainsheet can be modified to achieve the required jibstay sag.

VANG

Effect

Produces flexibility (gust and pitch responsiveness) by sagging the jibstay and by permitting the boom to rise readily to open the leech. Bends the lower mast, fore and aft, and, if boom is off the centerline, to windward thereby flattening the lower mainsail and loosening the jibstay; tightens or loosens the mainsail leech, depending upon the flexibility of the lower mast, and shifts draft aft; decreases side force but directs total force more aft; when used in place of mainsheet ("vang sheeting") eliminates need for traveler and functions in gust response to flatten main *(Fig. 3.5)*.

Initial Setting

Set to accommodate the lower luff curve of the mainsail (after basic curve achieved by permanent backstay tension, swept-back spreader pressure, jumper stay tension, deck level chocking, etc.).

Adjustment

Vang tension provides flexibility and should be applied in all dirty air conditions (erratic air flows, disturbed air, heavy air, and waves).

If the boom "floats" in these conditions (so that the mainsheet is under almost no tension and can be used as a traveler), the boom will rise and release the leech—produce more twist—in gusts and with pitching. The sagged jibstay will then flex instead of jerk. Both sails will retain attached flow despite marked variations in apparent wind strength and direction. Use of the vang may be the most important difference between smooth and rough water trim.

3.5. Vang. Note how vang tension bends the lower mast, sags the jibstay, and makes the boom end and leech more flexible.

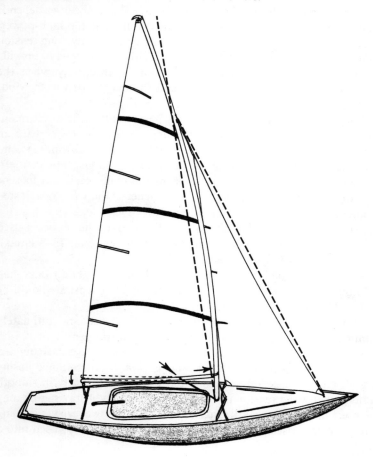

Vang tension when used as vang sheeting may be used in gust response. Tensioning the vang flattens the main and, depending upon the stiffness of the mast, either opens or closes the leech. Mast stiffness can be adjusted (by the use of struts, shroud/spreader relationships, chocking, etc.) so that the vang will effect the desired change in the leech. In a Laser with a very flexible mast, increased vang tension beneficially opens the leech; in a 5-0-5 with a properly adjusted mast strut, increased vang tension beneficially closes the leech in moderate air, but opens the leech in very heavy air. The effect upon the leech depends upon the degree to which the boom drives the lower mast forward and to windward and the degree to which the mast tip is twisted aft and to leeward as a consequence. Vang sheeting depends upon the presence of a mast sufficiently stiff that, for high-power, moderate air sailing, the upper leech can be brought by vang tension up to the stall. Increased flexibility can usually be arranged to provide leech opening when required in heavy air—particularly when the boom is trimmed off the centerline and the mast is driven to wind-ward.

Vang tension should usually be sufficient to flatten the lower main-sail in conformity with flow off the jib; that is, the lower mainsail should show minimal (but only minimal) lifting (backwinding) and the draft in the lower third of the mainsail should be 50 percent aft.

Vang tension either tightens or opens the main leech and loosens the forestay; both should be checked whenever the vang is adjusted (remember to modify the vang after a downwind leg).

When jibstay sag is less than desired (less than the jib being used was designed for), particularly in light to moderate air (3–8 knots), vang tension should be increased.

When jibstay sag is greater than desired, in very light air (less than 3 knots) and in moderate air (8–12 knots), vang tension should be reduced.

In very light air vang tension must be reduced and ultimately eliminated to permit the upper mainsail leech to open.

When sails of limited range are used, their ranges can be extended by setting them with and without vang tension. A full, minimal jibstay sag jib may be used into a high wind range, particularly in smooth water, when vang tension is minimal. A flat, high jibstay sag jib may be used into a low wind range, particularly in waves, when vang tension is increased. A flat, low mast bend main may be used into a high wind range, particularly in smooth water, when vang tension is minimal. A full, high mast bend main may be used into a low wind range, particularly in waves, when vang tension is increased.

As the boat enters a zone of increased waves where pitching will be increased (at the start, near marks, with increasing wind) or of more frequent gusts where changes in angle of incidence will be large, the vang should be tensioned and the mainsheet eased (proportionately) so as to permit the boom end and thus the leech to open with increases in wind velocity and with waves (which jar the rig). The vang may also be adjusted for gust control, that is, tensioned with each gust.

Whenever the vang is tensioned, the Cunningham must be tensioned and vice versa.

Beware of excessive vang tension, however, even in heavy air, as it may flatten the lower main (where the power should be retained), tighten the leech, move the mainsail draft aft, and slacken the jibstay excessively.

OUTHAUL

Effect

Flattens lower mainsail and moves draft of lower mainsail forward; opens lower leech (most important determinant); decreases side force *(Fig. 3.6)*.

Initial Setting

Set for designed foot shape of mainsail; optimal outhaul tension recognized when vertical wrinkles in foot are just removed and draft in lower mainsail is 50 percent aft. Unlike backstay, vang, and mainsheet, outhaul alters draft without affecting leech tension or jibstay tension.

Adjustment

Optimal outhaul tension (as indicated above), like mast bend, is appropriate to optimal boat speed conditions—smooth water, wind speed of 4–14 knots (dependent upon the boat and sail).

More outhaul tension is appropriate for all other conditions—particularly very light and very heavy air—when leeway is excessive.

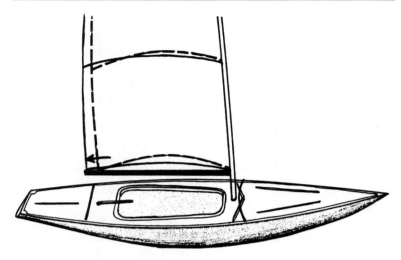

3.6. Outhaul. Note that outhaul tension decreases the mainsail fullness particularly in its lower portion.

Because the outhaul affects only the lower part of the sail, it should be tensioned sooner than the mast should be bent as the wind decreases from the optimal and it should be tensioned later than the mast should be bent as the wind increases from the optimal. (Fullness down low is tolerated better at higher wind velocities than is fullness aloft and is needed in waves.)

Outhaul tension is extremely important and should be susceptible to adjustment while hiking.

Outhaul should be eased, with the sail well twisted, in waves. Less tension is appropriate in heavy air when boom bending flattens the lower portion of the sail.

CUNNINGHAM (DOWNHAUL)

Effect

Moves draft in mainsail forward, thereby making leading edge fuller and leech flatter; decreases side force and directs total force more forward *(Fig. 3.7)*.

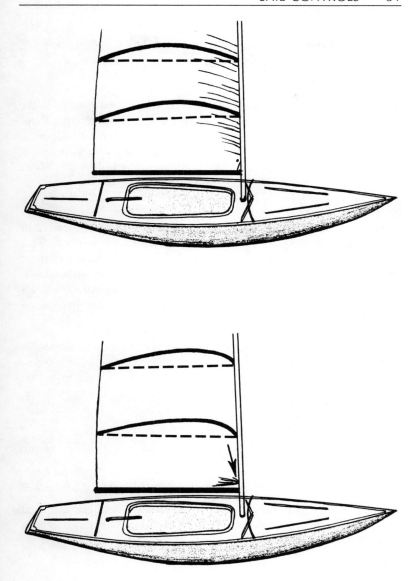

3.7. Cunningham. Note that Cunningham tension shifts the draft forward and flattens the leech.

Initial Setting

Set to keep position of maximum mainsail draft 50 percent aft; responsive control, continually adjusted.

Adjustment

Needs continual adjustment for variations in wind strength, above 12 knots, and for variations in backstay, vang, mainsheet, or outhaul tension, that is, for all changes in mast bend or mainsail fullness.

Between 4 and 12 knots with most mainsails, no adjustment of Cunningham is required; horizontal wrinkles which develop should be ignored unless mainsail draft moves aft of 50 percent.

Above 12 knots, tension is usually required to bring draft forward (up to the 50 percent position).

In strong winds, it may be necessary to move the draft forward of 50 percent, rounding up the luff and straightening the leech. This conformation creates a low leeway, low drag shape (when power must be reduced).

Waves require less Cunningham and less outhaul tension and less mast bend but more vang tension and more twist for a given wind strength.

MAIN TRAVELER

Effect

Alters angle of incidence (major determinant of total aerodynamic force and side force) and direction of total force produced (Fig. 3.8). Decreased sheeting angle (traveler car inboard) increases angle of incidence, increases total force and side force, directs total force more aft, and decreases drag angle (and vice versa).

Initial Setting

Set car so that boom is on centerline; highest pointing is achieved when drag angle is lowest, that is, when chord of sail is in line with heading. Lower sail chords should be approximately 4° above centerline, equal to the leeway angle.

Adjustment

Optimal setting (on centerline) is appropriate to optimal boat speed conditions: 4–14 knots, smooth water.

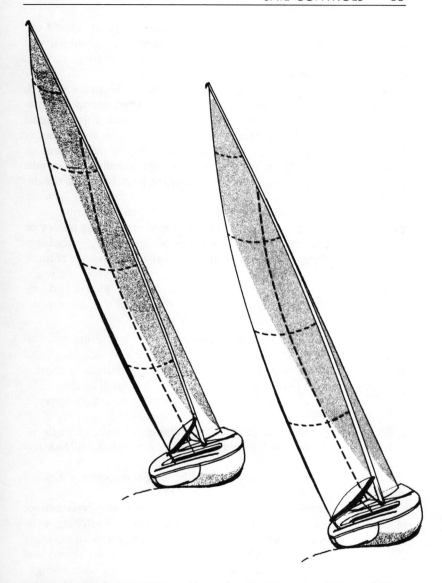

3.8. Main traveler. Note that, without changing the mainsail shape, shifting the traveler car to leeward opens the sail to decrease heeling force, increase driving force, and shift the center of effort forward.

Boom should be well to leeward of centerline in drifting conditions and in very heavy air (conditions in which speed is required to overcome leeway and high pointing is associated with slowing, stalling, and excessive leeway).

When steering is easy and pitching is minimal, the mainsail leech may be kept tight ("closed") and the entire sail/foil dropped to leeward, without any change in shape, with each gust or with a gradual increase in wind velocity. Heeling and yawing are prevented, leeway is reduced, and speed is increased at a slight loss in pointing.

In smooth water dropping the traveler is the best technique for gust control as the dramatic gusts of offshore (smooth water) winds require immediate responses.

Distances of boom to leeward and twist are a complementary couple: less distance means more twist, more distance means less twist. The advantage of a particular combination is dependent up air disturbance, vang/jibstay sag relationships, smoothness of water, etc.

MAINSHEET

Effect

Tensions main leech (decreases twist), thereby increasing mainsail fullness, moving draft aft, increasing total force and side force, and directing total force more aft; decreases drag angle, thereby improving pointing; tensions jibstay by pulling aft on mast tip *(Fig. 3.9)*.

Initial Setting

Set so as to position upper leech parallel to boom.

Keep lower leech telltales flowing and upper leech telltales just stalled.

Mainsheet (with traveler) or vang with "vang sheeting" is the major determinant of power (aerodynamic force).

Mainsheet tension directly affects twist; when the boat can be steered very accurately (little yawing) and there is little pitching, twist should be minimal; when the boat can only be steered with difficulty (marked yawing) and there is much pitching, twist should be maximal (to assure that some portion of the aerofoil is always functioning).

The mainsheet and the vang form a complementary couple: whenever the mainsheet is eased (so as to provide more twist), the vang should be tensioned. Whenever the vang is tensioned (so as to provide

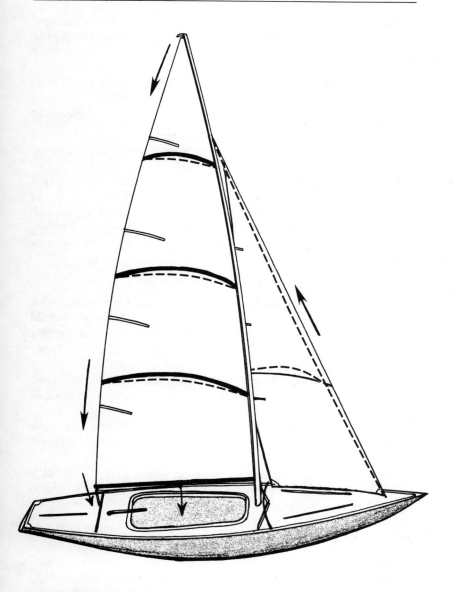

3.9. Mainsheet. Note the increase in leech tension, making the mainsail fuller, and the increase in jibstay tension, making the jib flatter.

more jibstay sag), the mainsheet should be eased. In waves (particularly in gusts) the mainsheet should be eased and the vang should be tensioned until the boom is "floating."

Adjustment

RESPONSIVE

In light air the mainsheet *must* be used for gust/lull control. Slight changes in wind velocity create major changes in force and therefore in leech tension (opening, twist), which must be counteracted by changes in mainsheet tension.

In gusts the classic response is "ease—hike—trim," meaning that the initial response is to ease the mainsheet and open the leech. In most boats and in most winds this is appropriate; opening the leech reduces both heeling and side force, thereby facilitating acceleration. (However, in some boats, adjusting the traveler, vang, or backstay may be more appropriate.)

INTENTIONAL

In waves, mainsheet tension should be reduced (compared with tension in smooth water at the same wind velocity). More twist should be provided whenever pitching is increased—in wakes, when tacking to a more up-wave tack—or if, in the presence of waves, wind velocity is reduced.

In moderate air and smooth water, when the boat is up to speed, minimal twist (upper batten parallel to boom) is essential to optimal performance and pointing.

In stronger winds (up to 18 knots?), if the water is smooth and the traveler is dropped to leeward (and used for gust control), minimal twist is appropriate.

Additional twist (or the negation of an otherwise closed leech) may be achieved in light air by lifting the boom (counteracting its weight) by hand, with a topping lift, with the spinnaker pole lift, etc.

JIBSTAY SAG

Significance

Jibstay sag is the most useful means of controlling jib shape. Sag primarily increases fullness (under almost all circumstances), usually rounds the entry of the sail, and commonly shifts the position of maximum draft forward. Jibsheet tension affects the leech as much or more than the fullness so that an increase in sheet tension undesirably tightens the leech as it flattens the sail, and a decrease in sheet tension twists (opens) the leech as it makes the sail fuller. Jib luff tension primarily rounds the entry, secondarily shifts the draft forward, flattens the leech, and decreases fullness. Because jibstay sag produces an increase in fullness in association with a rounding of the entry, it is the ideal means (better than the jibsheet or the luff tension) of increasing power and of making the jib more adaptable (to waves, dirty air, etc.). Because a reduction in jibstay sag produces a decrease in fullness in association with a flattening of the entry, it is the ideal means of decreasing power and improving pointing.

Except in two aspects, a genoa jib is affected no differently by jibstay sag than is a short-footed jib. Inasmuch as the effect of sag on fullness is inversely proportional to the chord length of the sail, the response of a genoa to jibstay sag varies with height and is greater aloft. A masthead genoa is characteristically set with a short halyard pennant and so its leech is not eased significantly as the jibstay sags. Thus, because all genoas become relatively fuller aloft and genoas with short halyard pennants ease the luff more than the leech, the leech of a masthead genoa tends to close as the jibstay sags—and requires that the sheet be eased. Genoas on fractional rigs with longer halyard pennants are less affected. Nonoverlapping jibs with long halyard pennants are usually affected in reverse; that is, their leeches are more eased than their luffs and their leeches tend to twist open.

Effect

The jibstay always sags to some degree. Its sag affects the jib's fullness, the position of its maximum draft, and its twist.

The precise effects depend upon:

The jib design and the jibsheet tension
The amount of sag
The wind velocity
The position of the head relative to the top of the jibstay (the length of the halyard pennant)

These factors determine whether the sag is aft or forward, to what extent the sag is to leeward, and to what extent the position of the leech is simultaneously altered.

The Jib Design and the Jibsheet Tension

The weight of the jibstay and the jib causes the jibstay to sag aft ("basic sag"). Tension in the jibsheet transmitted through the sail also pulls the jibstay aft. This effect will be increased if the jib is flat and particularly if its leading edge is flat. It will also be increased if its luff is cut with a curve greater than the basic sag and vice versa.

Amount of Sag

FACTORS INCREASING JIBSTAY SAG

Decreasing the aft tension on the mast
> Decreased permanent backstay or running backstay tension
> Decreased mainsheet tension

Lowering the site of jibstay attachment to the mast (bending the lower mast)
> "Pre-Bend": Chocking or pulling of the mast forward at the deck (or aft at the butt)
> Shroud/spreader relationships which pull the spreader tips and the mid-mast forward
> Trapeze attachment offset above the site of jibstay attachment which bends the mid-mast forward

Vang tension: Drives the boom and the lower mast forward at the gooseneck

Lateral mast bend: Sags the mid-mast to leeward and makes the mainsail fuller or bends the mid-mast to windward and makes it flatter
> Stiffening of the upper mast (jumper stays, etc.) causes the lower mast to bend more

Increasing the innate flexibility of the mast

FACTORS DECREASING JIBSTAY SAG

Increasing the aft tension on the mast
> Increased permanent backstay or running backstay tension
> Increased mainsheet tension

Raising the site of jibstay attachment to the mast (straightening the lower mast)
> Negative "pre-bend": Chocking or pulling of the mast aft at the deck (or forward at the butt)

Shroud/spreader relationships which pull the spreader
    tips and the mid-mast aft
Strut pressure (from the deck) which pushes the lower
    mast aft at the gooseneck
Trapeze attachment at the site of jibstay attachment (di-
    minishes "pre-bend")
Straightening the mast decreases lateral bend
Leading the lower shrouds aft and increasing their tension de-
    crease forward bend
Stiffening the lower mast (jumper stays, added external tracks,
    internal sleeves, etc.) and/or increasing the flexibility of the
    upper mast diminish lower mast bend
Increasing the innate stiffness of the mast

The Wind Velocity

Increased wind velocity increases jibstay sag and determines the
direction of the sag by increasing the tension in the jib luff. In strong
winds the luff tension pulls the jibstay chiefly to leeward. Aerodynamic lift tends to pull the luff forward (diminishing the "basic sag"
aft). In very strong winds with excessive sag, the jibstay may actually
sag forward.

Decreased wind velocity permits the "basic sag" effects to become
more evident: that is, in light air sag is chiefly aft, and in heavy air
it is chiefly to leeward.

The Position of the Jib Head

If the jib head is hoisted right to the mast, jibstay sag has very little
effect upon the leech. But, if the jib head is well down the stay (on
a long halyard pennant), as the jibstay sags, the jib head drops aft and
to leeward and the leech is eased (opened) and twisted.

Consequences of Jibstay Sag

Depending upon the net movement of both the stay and the leech,
the jib may become fuller or flatter, its draft may shift forward or aft,
and its leech may either open or close. Presuming that the jib design
and the length of the jib halyard pennant are fixed, control of jib shape
with variations in wind velocity requires modification of jibstay sag
(and jibsheet tension). Because the optimal jib shape varies with the

wind velocity, the optimal amount of jibstay sag also varies with the wind velocity—too much or too little will diminish the desired effect. The purposes of controlling jibstay sag are to:

1. Control jib fullness (which determines power and balance)
2. Control the distribution of maximum draft (which determines adaptation to dirty air and pointing)
3. Control the flexibility of the luff and leech (which determines adaptation to waves, irregularity of the airflow, and gusts)

Initial Setting

Use a jib whose luff is cut to match the jibstay sag considered to be optimal and achievable in the expected wind velocity. The main must, of course, be designed to accept the mast bend required to maintain this amount of jibstay sag. (Usually this means, in light air, a main with very little luff curve, requiring very little mast bend and permitting significant jibstay sag and, in heavy air, a main with marked luff curve, requiring marked mast bend and, through increased aft tension on the mast, limiting jibstay sag.)

Set the jibstay to sag the optimal mount and to match the jib luff curve. This usually means that in light air jibstay sag must be contrived, that in moderate air and smooth water jibstay sag is appropriate, that in heavy air jibstay sag must be decreased, and that in waves and dirty air jibstay sag must be increased.

Adjustment

LIGHT AIR *(Fig. 3.10)*

In light air when the jibstay sags, it sags aft, pushing the luff back into the sail. This increases the total fullness of the jib and particularly increases the fullness of the luff. The leech shifts aft and but minimally to leeward; it is slightly eased, flattened, and but minimally twisted. The net effect is that the sail is made fuller and that its draft is shifted forward. This trim facilitates attached flow (in a condition characterized by slow, erratic airflow which attaches with difficulty) and increases aerodynamic force (in a condition characterized by the need to produce power and speed).

In the absence of significant pressure on the sail, the rig tension required in most boats results in an excessively straight jibstay. Tech-

3.10. Jibstay sag—light air. Note that sag is chiefly aft and that the jib becomes fuller and its draft shifts forward.

niques which will increase jibstay sag must be applied. Usually decreasing aft tension on the mast (backstay and mainsheet tension) is insufficient or results in an inappropriate, draft-forward mainsail shape. The most satisfactory solution is to bend the mast below the site of jibstay attachment.

"Pre-bend," achieved by chocking, by mast-pulling, or by the shroud/spreader relationship, is the best technique because it permits the jibstay to sag without adversely affecting the mainsail shape; that is, it leaves the mainsail flat (which is essential in very light air).

The next best technique is the application of vang tension, which sags the jibstay but, in very light air, produces excessive main leech tension (i.e., undesirably increases mainsail fullness).

The third best technique is the creation of lateral mast bend (sag to leeward), but this only works when the wind is strong enough to sag the mast and it increases mainsail fullness.

0–3 knots: Use "pre-bend"—flattens mainsail

3–6 knots: Use "pre-bend" + vang tension—changes mainsail minimally as increased wind velocity opens leech

6–12 knots: Use lateral mast sag; discontinue "pre-bend" and vang tension—permits mainsail to become full

In some boats lateral mast sag should be maximal (to attain mainsail fullness and increase jibstay sag) at 4–6 knots, in others at 6–8 knots, and in still others at 8–10 knots. When pointing becomes more important than power, jibstay sag and lateral mast sag should be diminished. Maximum lateral sag can be in place in lighter air, 0–3 knots (with little effect), but should be progressively reduced above 8–10 knots (in smooth water).

MODERATE AIR *(Fig. 3.11)*

In moderate air, because the pressure on the sail is but moderate and the jibsheet tension (to keep the leech closed) is high, when the jibstay sags, it sags aft, making the jib fuller and shifting its draft forward. This shape is inappropriate to smooth water conditions. Once near-maximum speed has been reached (at around 8 knots), pointing becomes more important than additional speed. Pointing requires a fine entry, a flat jib luff, and a relatively flat jib with its draft aft. This must be attained by restricting the jibstay sag to an amount which matches the jib luff curve. If the sag can be reduced further, the jib luff will be pulled forward and beneficially become even flatter.

A decrease in jibstay sag in moderate air is best achieved by mainsheet tension, which tenses the jibstay (by pulling the mast aft) and closes the main leech (i.e., achieves the two essentials of pointing). At the same time the lower mast should be straightened: chocks, pullers, struts, and shroud/spreader relationships should be set for a straight mast, vang tension, should be eliminated, and lateral mast sag should be progressively reduced. The mast should be absolutely straight, with the least backstay tension, the fullest mainsail, and the straightest jibstay at the wind velocity which, despite maximum hiking, just begins to produce excessive heeling. Above this wind speed, increased backstay (mainsheet/vang tension) must be used to flatten the main-

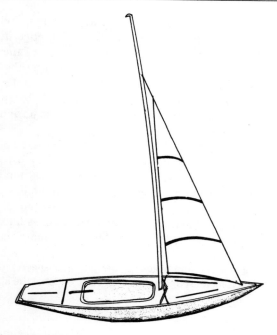

3.11. Jibstay sag—moderate air. Note that (in association with moderate mast bend and mainsheet tension typical of moderate air) jibstay sag is minimized and that the jib becomes flatter and its draft shifts aft.

sail, preserve or at least not increase jibstay sag, diminish heeling, and facilitate pointing.

HEAVY AIR *(Fig. 3.12)*

In heavy air because the pressure on, and the aerodynamic lift generated by, the sail is high, the jibstay sags to leeward and, with excessive sag, may even be blown forward. If the head is on a long halyard pennant, the leech will be eased and, as the head shifts aft and to leeward, will twist open. With moderate jibstay sag this easing and opening of the leech compensates for the aftwards shift of the draft due to sail stretch. But with excessive jibstay sag the luff flattens and the stay shifts forward, increasing the aftwards shift of the draft.

In heavy air, particularly in waves, with pitching, rolling, and yawing, a shift of the draft aft and a flat leading edge impair the initiation and maintenance of attached flow. A shift of the draft aft also results in a particularly deleterious gust response: the bow will be blown down, the angle of incidence will increase, and the boat will lay over and wallow instead of accelerating. Excessive jibstay sag must be decreased to shift the draft forward and permit the jib and the boat to adapt to waves and gusts.

The jibstay can be tensed, while the main is flattened, by permanent or running backstay tension (if available), pulling the mast aft. However, as the mast bend increases, the aft tension has less and less effect on the jibstay sag and the bending of the lower mast has more and more. The mainsheet is also less effective in heavy air because, to provide adaptability and flattening of the lower mainsail, much of its load must be transferred to the vang. The lower mast (unless it is

3.12. Jibstay sag—heavy air. Note that (despite mainsheet and backstay tension) jibstay sag is increased, chiefly to leeward, and that the jib becomes twisted and its draft shifts aft.

unusually stiff) cannot be prevented from bending, but its flexibility must be limited and the benefits of flattening the lower mainsail, through low mast bend, compromised. It should be stiffened to reduce the jibstay lowering and jibstay sag increasing effects of compressive bending, backstay loading, and vang tension by whatever means are available, including:

Negative "pre-bend": chocking, pulling, or strut use
   shroud/spreader relationships which pull the spreaders aft
Lower shrouds led aft and under increased tension
Stiffening the lower mast or making the upper mast more flexible

DIRTY AIR

In moderate air the optimal amount of sag depends upon the dirtiness of the air. In clear air and smooth water (as indicated above), when pointing is both desirable and feasible, the jibstay sag should be reduced—usually to the bare minimum, but at least to match the jib luff curve. However, in moderate but dirty air—disturbed by other boats, innately erratic, or affected by waves—jibstay sag must be increased proportionate to the degree of disturbance (relative to its clear air and smooth water optimum).

In moderate air increased jibstay sag increases the fullness of the jib and shifts the draft forward. These modifications are useful in initiating attached flow (difficult in dirty air) and in increasing power and speed (more important than pointing when speed is reduced and leeway is increased). In addition, moderate jibstay sag provides flexibility and permits the jib to adjust better to marked variations in the angle of incidence, the positions of its leech and luff, and its shape. In waves an excessively tight or an excessively loose jibstay jerks, changes the jib shape dramatically, and destroys attached flow. In disturbed air an excessively tight jibstay with its rigidly positioned air foil is unable to accommodate marked variations in the angle of incidence and therefore stalls readily.

A flexible jibstay and jib respond appropriately to variations in wind velocity and direction. The leech shifts off the centerline and decreases the angle of incidence whenever the wind velocity or the angle of incidence increases, and shifts toward the centerline and increases the angle of incidence whenever the wind velocity or the angle of incidence decreases. Transient increases in aerodynamic force are produced by the "pump effect" as the leech closes. Attached flow is maintained for a greater proportion of the total time; stalling is far less frequent.

JIB LUFF TENSION

Effect

Rounds entry (leading edge) and moves draft in jib forward, decreases side force and leeward yawing moment (in gusts), directs total force more forward, and facilitates attached flow *(Fig. 3.13)*.

Initial Setting

Set so as to keep position of maximum draft 35–50 percent aft. Jib differs from main in that, with variations in wind velocity (and pitching), far greater variations in jibstay sag occur than do variations in mast bend. Jib draft, like mainsail draft, tends to increase and move

3.13. Jib luff tension. Note that the jib draft shifts forward *and* that its leading edge becomes fuller with increased jib luff tension.

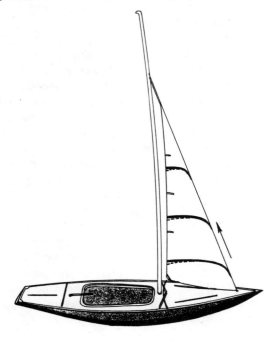

aft with increasing wind velocity (particularly with gusts). The jibstay sag which occurs simultaneously also tends to increase draft but causes it to move forward, counteracting the sail stretch. As a jib is used (grows older), its draft increases and moves aft particularly in its upper sections.

Adjustment

RESPONSIVE (DACRON SAILS)

With increasing wind velocity above 12 knots and particularly with gusts (and old jibs), luff tension must be increased (to counteract net aft movement of draft). Below 3 knots, the draft also moves aft because the tight jibstay flattens the leading edge. If jibstay sag cannot be arranged, some luff tension (sufficient to make the luff smooth) should be applied.

INTENTIONAL

In waves, when pitching and yawing make it difficult to maintain attached flow on the leading edge, the luff should be tensioned and the draft pulled forward (so as to eliminate horizontal wrinkles).

To increase power and improve pointing in moderate air and smooth water, the draft should be allowed to drift back (showing horizontal wrinkles).

Control of jib luff tension should be almost continuous: tension should be increased before starts, as the wind increases above 12 knots, as the boat tacks to a more up-wave tack, as she hits a wake, and as the wind diminishes below 4 knots. Tension should be decreased as the wind changes toward 4–12 knots, the boat tacks into smooth water, and reaches full speed following the start (a poor tack, hitting a wake, etc.).

Changes in tension should be accomplished with the halyard initially for waves—the luff tensed and the jib made fuller—and with the tack downhaul initially for velocity increases—the luff tensed and the jib made flatter (if these techniques are available).

MYLAR SAILS

Luff tension rounds the entry but has little effect upon fullness or position of maximum draft. Luff tension should be increased in proportion to wind strength only because increased wind strength is usually associated with waves.

JIB LEAD POSITION (FORE AND AFT)

Effect

Alters fullness, twist, and position of maximum draft. More vertical (forward on the boat) lead tensions the leech, decreases twist, moves position of maximum draft aft, and increases fullness, side force, and leeward yawing moment. More horizontal (aft on the boat) lead has the opposite effects *(Figs. 3.14A and 3.14B)*.

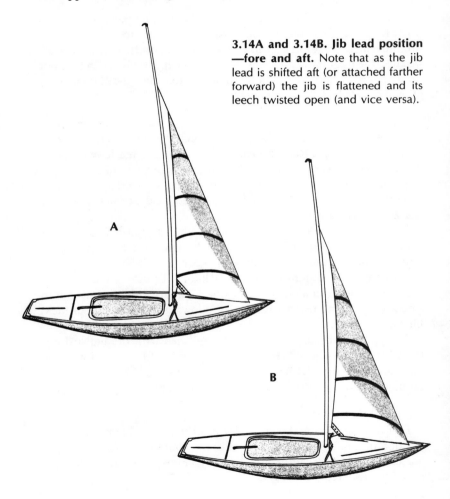

3.14A and 3.14B. Jib lead position —fore and aft. Note that as the jib lead is shifted aft (or attached farther forward) the jib is flattened and its leech twisted open (and vice versa).

A

B

Initial Setting

Set so that the jib luffs and stalls synchronously at all levels. The top of the jib must be considerably more open (twisted) than the bottom (shorter chords stall more easily and the wind is stronger with height). (In some boats this may mean that the top will luff before the bottom.)

Jib twist should always match mainsail twist (the jib leech with the leeward bulge of the main). One purpose of the jib is to diminish stalling and induced drag on the leeward surface of the main by directing organized airflow (chiefly from the leeward surface of the jib) tangentially onto the leeward surface of the main. Lifting of the main luff (slightly) demonstrates that this is occurring properly. The jib lead position, draft, and sheet tension should be adjusted to assure that this is happening.

Adjustment

Between 0 and 12 knots adjustment of jib shape can be accomplished adequately by alterations in sheet tension and luff tension. Above this wind strength, at least in smooth water, the lead may have to be moved aft to permit more sheet tension for the same twist.

Movement of the jib up or down the jibstay (if achievable) effectively changes the jib lead position and may obviate the need to make such changes throughout the range of use of any one jib, or if effected for other purposes (luff tension) may require a change in jib lead position (and/or a change in sheet tension).

If the jib lead position *is* changed, the sheet tension and the luff tension must be altered to be compatible; usually both must be eased as the lead is moved forward and vice versa.

Changes in rake require an alteration in jib lead position; if the rake is increased, the jib lead may need to be moved forward and vice versa.

JIB LEAD POSITION (LATERALLY)

Effect

Alters angle of incidence and therefore total force, side force, and direction of total force produced. Determines balance (by modifying the center of effort), gust response (yawing moment), and flow onto mainsail *(Fig. 3.15)*.

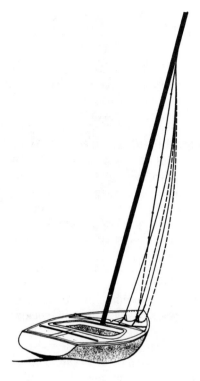

3.15. Jib lead position—laterally. Note that, without changing the jib shape, shifting the jib lead to leeward opens the sail to decrease heeling force, increase driving force, and shift the center of effort aft.

Initial Setting

Initial setting varies with hull, rig, and sails and can only be determined by testing with another boat. The optimal inboard position is appropriate to moderate air (4–14 knots).

Adjustment

Lateral jib lead position is extremely important, controlling as it does the angle of incidence of the jib plus the flow onto the main; slight adjustments make major differences in performance.

A shift outboard is appropriate to very light and very heavy air when boat speed is low relative to wind strength and leeway is increased.

If the main is to be kept untwisted in heavy air and the main traveler dropped to leeward (particularly in gusts), the jib lead must be shifted laterally to a lesser but proportionate degree. If, on the other hand, the main is to be twisted off (from a centerline traveler position), the jib lead need not be moved outboard as much. Place the jib lead so that the main luff lifts—but only slightly (when both sails are otherwise properly set).

Gust control requires chiefly that the jib leech be flat and that its draft be forward; however, strong gusts also require that the lead be moved outboard or that the leech be considerably twisted. If the lead is on a traveler (or similar), it should be played for gust control.

Lateral jib lead position determines pointing; if one needs to go higher, move it inboard; if one needs more speed and is willing to give up a little pointing, move it outboard.

JIBSHEET TENSION

Effect

Tensions jib leech (decreases twist) thereby increasing jib fullness, moving draft aft, increasing total force and side force, and directing total force more aft; decreases drag angle, thereby improving pointing; modifies flow onto mainsail; increases leeward yawing moment *(Figs. 3.16A and 3.16B)*.

Initial Setting

Set to bring jib leech into a parallel relationship with the leeward surface of the main.

Keep all leeward and leech telltales flowing.

Jibsheet tension is the most important adjustment on the boat (when going to windward); it should always be adjusted last—after everything else is "right." Slight alterations (¼ inch) make big differences in performance.

When in doubt—ease it!

Adjustment

RESPONSIVE

As the wind increases the jib clew tends to rise and the leech to twist; this must be counteracted by increasing jibsheet tension.

INTENTIONAL

In very light air, in very heavy air, and in gusts, as the main is allowed to twist, the jib must be allowed to do so (in conformity). In very light air a member of the crew should lift the clew in his hand to aid twist.

In waves, as yawing and pitching interfere with attached flow, the jibsheet should be eased so that some portion of the sail is always at an appropriate angle of incidence.

The jibsheet should always be eased in a lull, when tacking, when hitting a wake, when tacking to a more up-wave tack, and in disturbed air.

3.16A and 3.16B. Jibsheet tension. Note that with increased jibsheet tension the jib becomes fuller and its draft shifts aft.

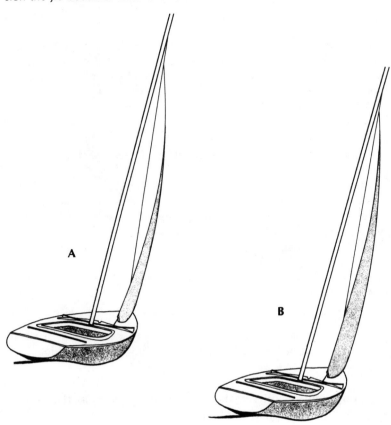

REACHING

RAKE (JIBSTAY LENGTH)

Effect

Alters center of effort and therefore yawing balance
Used to control the windward yawing moment created by trimming the boom outboard

Initial Setting

SPINNAKER-RIGGED BOATS

Leave rake in windward setting; spinnaker diminishes windward yawing moment making an alteration in rake unnecessary.

NON-SPINNAKER-RIGGED BOATS

Rake mast forward; rake forward counteracts the increase in windward yawing moment.

Adjustment

SPINNAKER-RIGGED BOATS

Leave rake aft until apparent wind is aft of abeam, then rake mast forward.

NON-SPINNAKER-RIGGED BOATS

Decrease rake progressively as boat is borne away and boom is trimmed progressively more outboard.

MAST BEND (FORE AND AFT AND LATERAL)

Effect

Fore-and-aft or lateral (to windward) bend flattens mainsail, moves position of maximum draft aft, and modifies power and balance. Adjust so as to maintain neutral helm.

Initial Setting

SPINNAKER-RIGGED BOATS

Reduce bend in light to moderate air.
Leave bend in windward setting for close reaching in heavy air; flattened mainsail diminishes windward yawing moment (which may, in heavy air, be excessive, despite the spinnaker).

NON-SPINNAKER-RIGGED BOATS

Leave bend in windward setting; flattened mainsail diminishes excessive windward yawing moment.

Adjustment

SPINNAKER-RIGGED BOATS

Decrease bend progressively as boat is borne away to an increasingly broad reach.

NON-SPINNAKER-RIGGED BOATS

Leave bend in windward setting until apparent wind is aft of abeam, then straighten mast.

VANG

Effect

Produces flexibility with the mainsheet tensioned; limits flexibility with the mainsheet eased. Controls twist, that is, angle of incidence of most of the mainsail (with the mainsheet eased), and therefore power. When under extreme tension, limits "pumping" of the mast (in a sea). Modifies yawing balance by altering power produced by main. Bends lower mast, sags jibstay, and flattens lower mainsail.

Initial Setting

Set to keep all mainsail leech telltales flowing. Tension until upper leech telltale drops and then ease until telltale flows (just short of stalling). Adjust in concert with main traveler and mainsheet to provide appropriate twist for conditions. Vang is the "fine-tuning" control for the leech in all conditions and total control when boom is beyond traveler.

Adjustment

Ease, to increase twist, as wind velocity decreases; tension, to decrease twist, as wind velocity increases (after setting main traveler and mainsheet).

Ease, in waves, when steering is difficult; tension in smooth water, when steering is easy (after setting main traveler and mainsheet).

Play in heavy air to keep mainsail at optimal angle of incidence, to keep boat at an appropriate angle of heel, to balance windward yawing moment, and to prevent broaching.

OUTHAUL

Effect

Flattens lower mainsail and moves draft forward thereby altering power and yawing balance.

Initial Setting

Set for maximum draft for which mainsail was designed. Ease until vertical wrinkles appear and position of maximum draft is 50 percent aft.

Adjustment

Optimal outhaul tension (as indicated above) is appropriate to light and moderate air.

In moderate air, tension sufficiently so that flow off the jib does not produce excessive backwinding.

In heavier air, tension until heeling and windward yawing moment are controlled or until the foot is stretched to the black band.

CUNNINGHAM

Effect

Moves draft in mainsail forward. Modifies power and particularly side force, thereby affecting yawing balance.

Initial Setting

Set to keep the position of maximum draft 50 percent aft (for greatest efficiency).

Adjustment

Optimal Cunningham tension (as indicated above) is appropriate to moderate air.

In lighter air, it may be difficult to keep the draft sufficiently far aft even with Cunningham fully eased. Ease the main halyard or bend the mast fore and aft or laterally (to windward) if necessary.

In heavier air, tension so as to reduce side force and heeling and windward yawing moment.

MAIN TRAVELER

Effect

Alters sheeting angle, angle of incidence, and particularly side force.

Initial Setting

Set to keep all mainsail leech telltales flowing at the appropriate degree of adaptability and twist for the conditions; that is, traveler car more to leeward to create less twist (less vang, more mainsheet) in smooth water, traveler car more to windward to create more twist (more vang, less mainsheet) in waves. Traveler car position is the primary setting to determine reaching twist, followed by mainsheet and vang.

Adjustment

Ease (to leeward) as boat is borne away, as wind velocity increases, and as water becomes smoother.

Tension (to windward) as boat heads higher, as wind velocity decreases, and as water becomes rougher.

Play in light and moderate air and in smooth water and heavy air to keep mainsail at optimal angle of incidence, to keep boat at appropriate angle of heel, and to balance windward yawing moment.

MAINSHEET

Effect

Tensions main leech. Controls twist (in conjunction with vang). Modifies draft, position of maximum draft, and yawing balance.

Initial Setting

Set to keep all mainsail leech telltales flowing (just short of stalling) in conjunction with vang. When close reaching, mainsheet *can* control leech and in light to moderate air and in smooth water should be used with minimal vang tension. When boat is borne away, mainsheet rapidly becomes ineffective in controlling leech (functions only as a traveler when boom is beyond the traveler). Vang should control leech in waves, in heavy air, and when the boom is beyond the traveler.

Adjustment

Ease as boat is borne away and vice versa.

Ease to increase twist as wind velocity decreases; tension to decrease twist as wind velocity increases (when mainsheet is controlling leech).

Transfer tension to vang when more twist is desired, to mainsheet (when close reaching) when less twist is desired.

JIBSTAY SAG

Effect

As mast is straightened and allowed to rake forward, jibstay sag is increased.

Sag aft increases draft and moves it forward. Sag to leeward increases draft and moves it aft.

Initial Setting

Set (consistent with mast bend appropriate to mainsail and vang tension appropriate to mainsail twist) so as to sag as much as possible without "pumping," that is, so as to increase power maximally. Increased power from jib increases total driving force and corrects windward yawing moment.

Adjustment

No adjustment is required ordinarily. Increase sag if jib is too flat. Decrease sag if "pumping" develops. Then tension jibstay (rather than backstay), if possible, so that decrease in rake will assist in counteracting windward yawing moment.

JIB LUFF TENSION

Effect

Shifts draft in jib forward, reduces draft by flattening leech, and facilitates attached flow.

Initial Setting

Set to keep draft in jib 50 percent aft from leading edge. As jibstay sag is increased, jib luff tension must be reduced so as to keep draft from moving forward.

Adjustment

Ease if draft moves forward and/or horizontal wrinkles along luff disappear. Tension if draft moves aft excessively, particularly in waves, when steering is difficult and a full leading edge is necessary to maintain attached flow.

JIB LEAD POSITION (FORE AND AFT)

Effect

Controls vertical distribution of draft and twist.

Initial Setting

Shift forward of upwind position (if possible) so as to reduce twist associated with easing jibsheet.

Adjustment

Modify (if possible) so as to keep the draft of all horizontal sections approximately the same and all telltales stalling and luffing simultaneously.

JIB LEAD POSITION (LATERAL)

Effect

Alters angle of incidence, yawing balance, gust response, and flow onto mainsail.

Initial Setting

Shift to leeward of upwind position (if possible) so as to prevent stalling (of after sections), improve gust response (avoid the bow being blown to leeward), reduce twist, and assure that flow off the jib flows tangentially onto the leeward surface of the main. Set so that all leech telltales are flowing.

Adjustment

Modify with alterations in heading, wind velocity, or direction so as to maintain the effects indicated above.

JIBSHEET TENSION

Effect

Tensions jib leech (decreases twist) thereby altering draft, position of maximum draft, angle of incidence, gust response, yawing balance, and flow onto mainsail.

Initial Setting

Ease so as to keep all leeward surface telltales just short of stalling.

Adjustment

Trim until leeward telltales begin to stall (fall) and then ease until they flow continuously (just short of stalling). Particularly on a non-spinnaker-rigged boat, play jibsheet continuously to keep jib just short of stalling. Attempt the best compromise (if necessary) to keep the greatest area of the jib at the appropriate angle of incidence (top luffing, bottom stalled).

SPINNAKER HALYARD

Effect

Transmits power of spinnaker to boat (along with guy and sheet).

Initial Setting

Hoist spinnaker to maximum height.

Adjustment

Ease in moderate air and smooth water so as to permit spinnaker to separate from disturbance due to mainsail and mast. Keep fully hoisted in light air and in heavy air or waves so as to stabilize spinnaker *(Figs. 3.17A and 3.17B)*. (The spinnaker, attached to the boat only at its corners, is inherently unstable. Maintenance of attached flow depends upon keeping it full *and* fixed relative to mast and hull.)

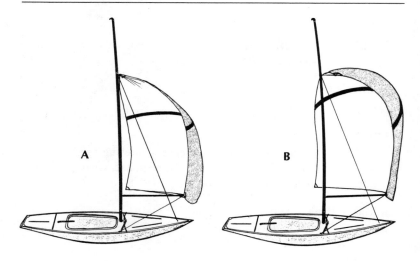

3.17A and 3.17B. Spinnaker halyard. Note the need to hoist the halyard fully in light air (A) and the advantages of easing it in moderate air (B).

SPINNAKER POLE POSITION—HORIZONTAL (GUY)

Effect

Alters angle of incidence, draft, position of maximum draft, heeling, gust response, and yawing balance *(Fig. 3.18)*.

Initial Setting

Set so that luff of spinnaker is folding in (luffing) when remainder of sail is at optimal (designed) draft.

Adjustment

Trim guy (aft) until luff of spinnaker begins to collapse. If spinnaker is now too flat, ease guy and sheet (forward); if spinnaker is now too full, tension guy and sheet (aft).

Tension guy whenever boat is borne away, wind shifts aft, or boat speed diminishes—and vice versa.

Tension guy to decrease heeling and windward yawing moment and improve gust response.

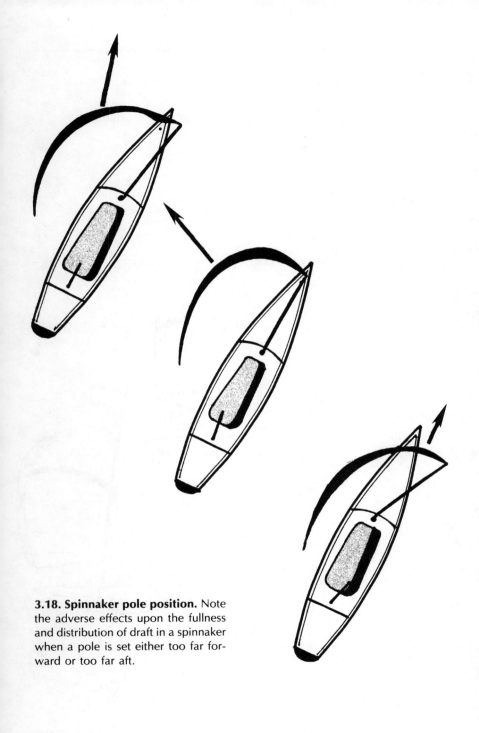

3.18. Spinnaker pole position. Note the adverse effects upon the fullness and distribution of draft in a spinnaker when a pole is set either too far forward or too far aft.

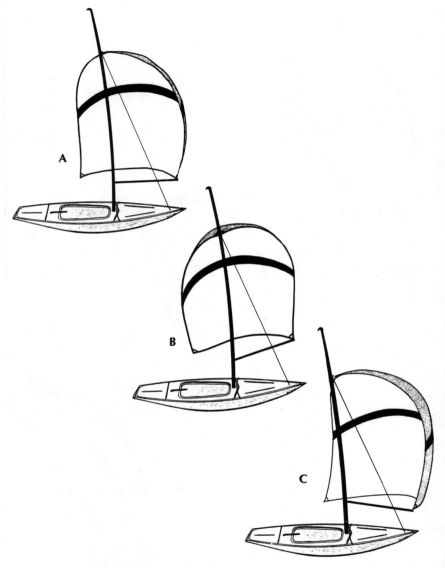

3.19A–3.19C. Spinnaker pole heights. Note the adverse effects upon the distribution of draft in a spinnaker when a pole is set either too high or too low.

SPINNAKER POLE POSITION—VERTICAL

Effect

Modifies twist of both leech and luff (elevation increases luff twist and decreases leech twist—and vice versa) and alters draft, position of maximum draft, gust response, and yawing balance *(Figs. 3.19A–3.19C)*.

Initial Setting

Set pole so that tack is at same height (above the deck) as the clew, so that the twists of both luff and leech are the same and the shapes of the two vertical halves of the spinnaker are the same. The pole should always be set within 15° of horizontal; otherwise the projection of the spinnaker is diminished.

Adjustment

When the wind shifts aft or decreases in velocity or the boat is borne away, the luff will sag into a "J" shape, the clew will drop, the leech will straighten, and the draft will move aft. The pole should then be lowered to tension the luff, equalize the twist, and restore the draft to the mid-position. When in the opposite conditions (the luff tightens, the clew rises, the leech twists, and the draft moves forward), the pole should be raised.

Lowering the pole will shift the draft forward, decrease heeling, decrease the weather yawing moment, and improve gust response— and vice versa.

SPINNAKER SHEET LEAD

Effect

Alters twist, draft, and distribution of draft of the spinnaker *(Figs. 3.20A and 3.20B)*.

Initial Setting

Lead spinnaker sheet as far laterally as possible so as to spread (and flatten) spinnaker as much as possible. (When close reaching, almost all spinnakers are too full.) Lead to boom end or around mainsail leech (above boom) if possible (so long as pole is within approximately 30° of the forestay). Lead as far aft as possible and, for close reaching,

3.20A and 3.20B. Spinnaker sheet lead position. Note the adverse effect upon the distribution of draft of a lead that is too far forward.

as high as possible so as to keep leech open and twisted. If legal, sheet should be led to a block mounted on a pedestal above the deck (to match the pole/guy effect).

Adjustment

Move lead down and forward as the boat is headed lower. When bearing away with the pole more than approximately 30° off the forestay, be prepared (by releasing vang and lifting boom over sheet) to shift sheet to a position below the boom.

SPINNAKER SHEET

Effect

Alters angle of incidence and draft directly and heeling, gust response, and yawing balance with each adjustment *(Fig. 3.21)*.

Initial Setting

Set in relation to pole position (guy) so that luff is collapsing regularly with spinnaker at optimal draft. Should be trimmed continu-

3.21. Spinnaker sheet tension. Note the critical effect of spinnaker sheet tension upon airflow attachment.

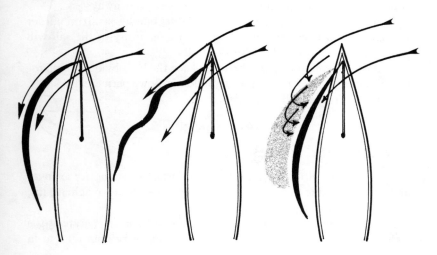

ously to keep luff collapsing. (The only means of determining that the luff is at the optimal angle of incidence and the flow at the leading edge is attached is to demonstrate that the luff is collapsing regularly.)

Adjustment

"When in doubt, ease the sheet." Ease when the boat is borne away, the wind shifts aft, the wind velocity diminishes, the boat slows (on the back of a wave), the luff sags, and whenever the trimmer looks away. Tension when the boat is headed up, the wind shifts forward, the wind velocity increases, the boat speeds up (on the face of a wave), and when the luff collapses excessively. Always keep the sheet eased and the luff collapsing because, if the spinnaker stalls, it may be very difficult (by pushing the sheet?) to initiate attached flow and get it full again. If the sheet is eased too much and the sail collapses (by luffing) it will be easy to reinitiate attached flow by trimming, but remember that it is necessary to overtrim in order to overcome collapse. Immediately after overtrimming the sheet must be eased until the luff is collapsing again.

Ease the sheet to the maximum acceptable degree of luff collapse whenever the boat heels, drives into the back of a wave, appears to wish to "round up," develops excessive weather helm, or is hit by a gust. Let the sheet go so as to collapse the spinnaker if the initial ease is insufficient to prevent the boat from broaching; that is, if increased rudder angulation does not cause the boat to bear away.

In moderate air and smooth water (stable) conditions, trim harder so that the luff is barely collapsing and the majority of the sail will generate more power, closer to the stall.

In unstable conditions, it is better to keep the luff obviously collapsing because, if the sail, in the variable air flow, periodically stalls, power will dramatically diminish.

RUNNING

AERODYNAMIC FORCES

Aerodynamic lift always produces additional driving force (over and above that due to drag); so, whenever it is possible to achieve lift, it should be arranged *(Fig. 3.22).*

In most running conditions the mainsail and the jib operate at the stall (producing drag without lift). However, in very light air and in

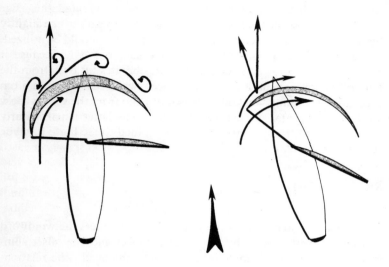

3.22. Aerodynamic force—running. Note airflow around spinnaker at the stall and lift generated near luff when the boat is headed up.

3.23. Aerodynamic force—running. Note airflow over spinnaker and lift generated near head.

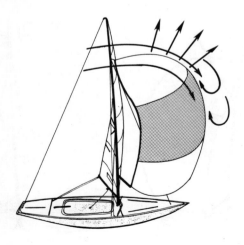

heavy air-planing conditions, they should be so trimmed and the boat should be so headed that aerodynamic lift is also created.

When it is possible (by "tacking downwind"), by sailing at a slightly higher sailing angle, to create lift, that higher angle should be utilized. The spinnaker is a particularly valuable sail, not only because it provides such a large area, but because it generates lift both from the horizontal flow around its vertical surfaces (while reaching and broadreaching, including "tacking downwind") and from the vertical flow above its horizontal surfaces (at all times). The latter is particularly important, and the spinnaker must be trimmed to facilitate it, while running *(Fig. 3.23)*.

RAKE (JIBSTAY LENGTH)

Effect

Alters the center of effort; forward rake counteracts the windward yawing moment created by the offset mainsail and the offset spinnaker. Determines the angle of incidence of the head—the relationship between the horizontal surfaces of the spinnaker and the air flowing over (above) them *(Figs. 3.24A and 3.24B)*.

3.24A and 3.24B. Yawing balance. Note the improvement in yawing balance achieved by raking the mast forward.

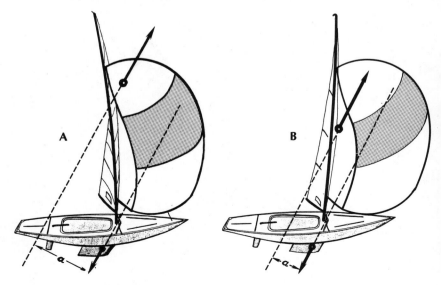

Initial Setting

Rake forward of vertical (if possible) until the windward yawing moment is balanced. In non-spinnaker-rigged boats, forward rake is particularly important (because the windward yawing moment due to the offset boom is not counteracted by a spinnaker).

In spinnaker-rigged boats, it is additionally useful because it separates the spinnaker from the mainsail, greatly improving the efficiency of the partially blanketed spinnaker. The aerodynamic lift created by the air flowing above the spinnaker, the angle of incidence, and the lift are increased by forward rake.

Adjustment

No adjustment is ordinarily necessary. Usually, it is impossible to rake the mast sufficiently far forward. Every effort should be made to increase the rake until the helm is balanced and maximum lift is achieved.

MAST BEND

Effect

Initial bend due to compressive forces may be abruptly increased as the spinnaker fills and therefore, in heavy air, is hazardous. However, if the mainsail is cut with a large luff round, some residual mast bend (fore and aft or lateral) may be desirable to keep the mainsail draft properly distributed.

Initial Setting

Before the mast is raked forward and the spinnaker set, release the backstay, Cunningham, mast ram, or other mast bending device and, in heavy air, ensure that the mast is supported in a manner that will permit it to remain nearly straight.

In moderate air, provide moderate lateral flexibility which will permit the mainsail luff round to be approximately matched.

VANG

Effect

Controls twist (leech tension) and mainsail fullness (through low mast bend) as the gooseneck is driven forward and to windward.

Facilitates compressive mast bend.

Initial Setting

Ease (if under tension on previous leg) the vang to reduce compressive mast bend. Retain sufficient tension so that the mainsail has only minimal twist (avoiding excess fullness and the creation of a lateral rolling force aloft) and so that the mast is not bent (to windward or forward) excessively.

Adjustment

If a lateral roll develops, increase the vang tension to reduce the mainsail twist. If compressive mast bending seems excessive, reduce the tension. If the boat (in light or heavy air) can be sailed sufficiently high so as to generate mainsail lift, the vang should be adjusted so as to keep the leeward surface and, if possible, the leech telltales flowing.

OUTHAUL

Effect

When eased, the outhaul increases the fullness of the lower mainsail.

A full sail impedes the airflow (increases static pressure, creates more drag) better (but only slightly better) than a flat one; that is, downwind produces more force operating in the desired direction.

Initial Setting

Ease until the tension along the foot is relieved (so as to create maximum fullness) but, to avoid diminishing the projected area of the mainsail, no further.

CUNNINGHAM

Effect

When eased, the Cunningham increases the fullness of the mainsail, allows the draft to move aft, and relieves some of the compressive mast bending.

Initial Setting

Should be released completely so as to allow the draft to shift aft (i.e., so as to prevent it from shifting forward as the mast is straightened).

MAINSHEET

Effect

Acts as a traveler to alter the sheeting angle (the vang controls the vertical movement of the boom) and the projected area. (Downwind the projected area is the major determinant of the driving force.)

Initial Setting

Ease until the boom is approximately perpendicular to the apparent wind. (When within 15° of this position, the projected area varies minimally.)

In heavy air, easing the boom to approximately 70° off the centerline provides almost full projection of area while diminishing the likelihood of excessive rolling.

Adjustment

Needs little adjustment (except in heavy air to reduce rolling) so long as the sail is operating at the stall. If, however (particularly in light air when "tacking" downwind), the apparent wind shifts far enough forward to produce attached flow, the boom must be trimmed in, so as to achieve an appropriate angle of incidence with the leech telltales flowing or just stalled. A major increase in driving force results from such trim, which should always be sought in light air.

JIBSHEET TENSION

Effect

In spinnaker-rigged boats, as the mast is raked forward, the jibstay becomes slack, and the jib is blanketed behind the main. Lead position, luff tension, etc., are thus of little significance. Jib trim is dependent almost entirely upon jibsheet tension. Overlapping jibs ordinarily must be dropped when the spinnaker is set. Nonoverlapping jibs may be used effectively in moderate to heavy air. Then their trim (angle of incidence, fullness, twist, draft distribution, etc.) is dependent upon jibsheet tension.

Initial Setting

Ease the jibsheet completely at the commencement of the run; if the jib stalls early in the process of bearing away, eddy formation may interfere with the setting of the spinnaker. Shift the jib lead as far laterally as possible and keep the jibsheet eased to present the greatest possible projected area.

In light air and whenever sailing at an angle which permits the generation of lift, keep the jibsheet sufficiently eased so that the jib is not stalled, and so that its leech telltales are flowing.

SPINNAKER HALYARD

Effect

Controls the exposure of the spinnaker. The head tends to fly horizontally, the foot vertically. By easing the halyard, the angle of incidence of the upper portion of the sail can be increased. If this does not result in a greater portion of the sail being stalled, an increase in driving force should result.

Initial Setting

Ease the halyard so that the head of the spinnaker is approximately 1 foot from the mast and/or until the foot begins to curve back toward the boat. This should provide the optimal angle of incidence for the generation of lift. The halyard should be eased more if the mast cannot be raked forward, less if it can be.

Adjustment

Hoist the halyard progressively higher (until two-blocked) as the wind increases above 12–14 knots or decreases below 4–6 knots.

The spinnaker should be fully hoisted in heavy air to prevent oscillation and in light air to elevate the sail into the stronger airflow. The halyard should also be fully hoisted as the boat is sailed at higher sailing angles (tacking more widely downwind).

SPINNAKER POLE POSITION—VERTICAL

Effect

Modifies twist, exposure (shift to windward of mast), and distribution of the draft of the spinnaker *(Fig. 3.25).*

Initial Setting

Set the pole horizontally (or within 15° of horizontal) and at a height which causes the spinnaker to set symmetrically: the center seam should be vertical, the clew at the same height as the tack, the luff breaking initially aloft, and most of the sail exposed to windward of the mast. (Heeling the boat slightly to windward and bow down will help to shift the spinnaker to windward.)

Adjustment

The pole height should be adjusted frequently, particularly in light air, to keep the spinnaker setting symmetrically.

In light to moderate air, when in doubt, set the pole lower than the clew to encourage the spinnaker to swing to windward. When the spinnaker does swing to windward and the clew lifts, the pole should be elevated to restore symmetry. The pole should also be raised progressively as the boat heads higher and is usually fully hoisted when tacking downwind at wide angles.

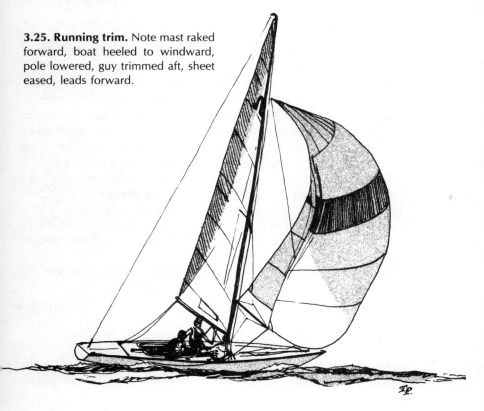

3.25. Running trim. Note mast raked forward, boat heeled to windward, pole lowered, guy trimmed aft, sheet eased, leads forward.

SPINNAKER POLE POSITION—HORIZONTAL (GUY)

Effect

Modifies the exposure (shift of the spinnaker to windward of the mast) and the draft of the spinnaker.

Initial Setting

Set to position the pole approximately perpendicular to the air flow with the spinnaker exposed as far as possible to windward of the mast. When the guy is set properly, the sheet should keep the luff on the verge of collapse without unduly flattening the spinnaker. This usually happens when the foot is positioned just outside the forestay.

Adjustment

In the absence of a major change in velocity, no adjustment is appropriate. The boat should be steered so that the spinnaker, trimmed to the fixed pole, is always at the proper angle of incidence (its luff just on the verge of collapsing).

When the apparent wind velocity changes, the guy (and the pole position) should be altered. As the wind increases and the optimal sailing angle becomes lower, the guy should be trimmed aft and the boat headed lower (and vice versa). The guy should also be altered to permit a change in course appropriate to getting into and remaining in streaks of stronger air. It should also be altered as necessary to deal with tactical requirements: blanketing, escape from blanketing, etc.

Downwind the guy is, therefore, the most important trim control. The boat is steered to maintain a constant angle of incidence with a fixed guy unless the true wind strength changes (or the boat jibes into a different wind) or the course is changed (for tactical or strategic reasons).

If the wind direction changes, the heading is altered, the guy remains fixed, and, if appropriate, the boat is jibed.

SPINNAKER SHEET LEAD

Effect

Alters the twist, draft, and distribution of draft of the spinnaker.

Initial Setting

Lead the spinnaker sheet as far laterally as possible, so as to spread the spinnaker as widely as possible. Lead the sheet down to the deck or gunwhale approximately amidships (under the main boom), so as to keep the clew from rising above the tack and so as to keep the leech from twisting.

The spinnaker should be kept symmetrical and full in all of its horizontal sections.

Adjustment

Move the lead aft (ease the twing, if used to control the lead) as the boat is headed higher. When reaching with the pole less than 30° off the forestay, the sheet should be shifted to a position above the boom.

SPINNAKER SHEET

Effect

Alters the angle of incidence and draft of the spinnaker.

Initial Setting

Ease until the luff begins to collapse and then trim just enough to reverse the collapse. The angle of incidence varies continually with changes in wind direction, wind velocity, or boat speed; therefore (when sailing at angles of incidence producing lift), the sheet must be trimmed continuously to keep the greatest possible area unstalled.

When sailing more directly downwind (stalled), the sheet must be eased until the maximum possible exposure has been achieved and periodically eased further to test this state.

Adjustment

When oscillation must be prevented and/or when steering is easy, keep the sail flattened and spread maximally across the boat by trimming both the sheet and the guy.

In light air and in waves when collapse is likely and/or steering is difficult, keep the sail full by easing the sheet and the guy forward.

Whenever the spinnaker luff begins to sag (because the wind velocity diminishes or because the wind shifts aft), the boat must be headed higher and the sheet eased.

Whenever the spinnaker fails to sag, the sheet should be eased and the boat worked down toward the rhumb line.

In light to moderate air, this can only be achieved by intermittent testing. If the sheet trimmer keeps the luff collapsing continuously, the helmsman can, without reducing the spinnaker's exposure, periodically bear away and trim the guy aft (to test how low he can sail).

The boat can be sailed lower without reducing the spinnaker's exposure when:

1. The mast is raked forward
2. The boat is heeled to windward and bow down
3. The pole is as low as the clew
4. The guy is trimmed as far aft as possible and trimmed further aft when the boat bears away
5. The sheet is eased to keep the luff collapsing continuously and eased further as soon as and whenever the boat is borne away

4
Crew Movement Techniques

EFFECT

Rapid movement of the crew (displacement of the weight of the crew) may alter the angle of incidence and the pressure upon the sails (i.e., alter the apparent wind and the aerodynamic lift) and may alter the angle of incidence and the pressure upon the keel and rudder (i.e., alter the water flow and the hydrodynamic lift).

PRINCIPLES

Crew movement techniques may be used (within the limitations of Rule 54—see below) to steer the boat (and thereby diminish the drag which would otherwise result from rudder angulation) and to increase the apparent wind and decrease the underwater resistance, thereby maintaining or increasing speed when turning, surfing, and initiating planing.

RULE 54: MEANS OF PROPULSION

54.1: BASIC RULE

(a) Unless otherwise permitted by this rule, a yacht shall be propelled only by the natural action of the wind on the sails and spars, and the water on the hull and underwater surfaces. A yacht shall not check way by abnormal means.

(b) Sails may be adjusted and a competitor may move his body in order to change the angle of heel or fore-and-aft trim, or to facilitate steering. However, except as provided in rules

54.1(c) and 54.3, no actions, including *tacking* and *gybing*, shall be performed which propel the yacht faster than if the sails, hull, and underwater surfaces had been trimmed to best advantage at the time.

(c) A yacht may promote or check way by means other than those permitted by this rule for the purpose of Rule 58 (Rendering Assistance).

(d) A yacht may anchor as permitted by Rule 63 (Casting Off, Anchoring, Making Fast, and Hauling Out) and Rule 64 (Aground or Foul of an Obstruction). A yacht shall not recover an anchor in a manner that causes her to pass the point at which the anchor is lifted off the ground.

54.2: ACTIONS THAT ARE PROHIBITED

Examples of actions which are prohibited except as permitted under rules 54.1(b) or 54.3:

(a) Repeated forceful movement of the helm (sculling).

(b) Persistent or rapidly repeated trimming and releasing of any sail (pumping).

(c) Sudden movement of the body forward or aft (ooching).

(d) Persistent or rapidly repeated vertical or athwartships body movement.

(e) Movement of the body or adjustment of the sails or centerboard which lead to persistent rolling of the yacht (rocking).

54.3: ACTIONS THAT ARE PERMITTED

The following actions are permitted for the sole purpose of accelerating a yacht down the face of a wave (surfing), or when planing conditions exist, responding to an increase in the velocity of the wind.

(i) No more than three rapidly repeated trims and releases of any sail (pumping).

(ii) Sudden movement of the body forward or aft (ooching).

There shall be no further pumping or ooching with respect to that wave or increase of wind.

TECHNIQUES INTENDED TO INCREASE THE APPARENT WIND—CONSISTENT WITH RULE 54

UPWIND

Rocking ("unweighting," "slamming," "power hiking") *(Fig. 4.1)*

Apparent wind abruptly increases and shifts aft.

Attached flow persists temporarily despite the increase in the angle of incidence and lift increases.

Recovery is achieved by a gradual return to the initial position.

(Rocking once is always permissible; persistent or rapidly repeated rocking which leads to persistent rolling is prohibited.)

Roll Tacking (combination of rocking and turning)

Apparent wind abruptly increases and shifts aft in both the initial and recovery phases.

Attached flow persists despite turning the boat into the wind as the angle of incidence is kept high throughout most of the tack and lift increases.

Recovery is achieved by a reverse rock on the opposite tack.

4.1. Rocking. Note forces involved in rocking and changes in apparent wind which result.

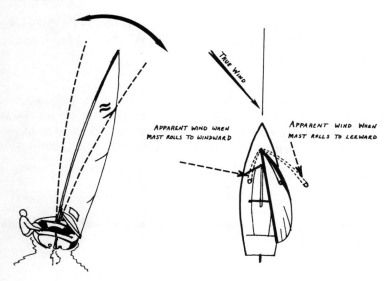

OFFWIND

Rocking (rolling) *(Fig. 4.2)*

Apparent wind increases and shifts forward.

Attached flow is created (from the stalled state) or enhanced and lift increases.

Recovery is achieved by reversing the flow in a reverse rock.

Driving force (acting forward) is attained from the lift generated during both phases of the roll.

Roll Jibing (combination of rocking and turning)

Apparent wind increases and shifts forward.

Attached flow is created or enhanced and lift increases.

Recovery is achieved by a reverse rock on the opposite jibe.

Pumping (the "pump effect") *(Fig. 4.3)*

Apparent wind increases and shifts aft.

Attached flow persists temporarily despite the increase in the angle of incidence and lift increases.

Recovery is achieved by a gradual return of the sail to its initial position.

(One pump is permissible at any time. Persistent or rapidly repeated pumping is only permitted [three times] to initiate surfing or planing.)

TECHNIQUES INTENDED TO DECREASE THE WATER RESISTANCE—CONSISTENT WITH RULE 54

UPWIND

Torquing

During wave traverses underwater resistance (both frictional and wave-making of both the hull and the rudder) is diminished (comparatively) and lift from the rudder is maintained as the boat is steered by body movement and alterations in immersion.

Heeling (while turning)

During tacks, mark roundings, and other turns, underwater resistance is diminished (comparatively) and lift from the rudder is maintained as the boat is steered by body movement and alterations in immersion.

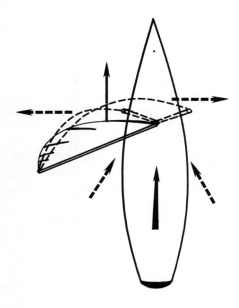

4.2. Rolling. Note creation of aerodynamic force acting laterally with each element of the roll.

4.3. Pumping. Note increase in aerodynamic force and preservation of attached flow with pump.

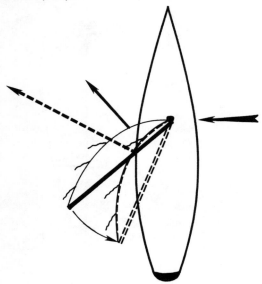

OFFWIND

Torquing and Heeling (while wave-riding)

Underwater resistance is diminished and lift from the rudder is maintained as the boat is steered by body movement.

Ooching *(Fig. 4.4)*

Spray resistance is abruptly diminished as the fore-and-aft trim angle is altered (particularly if it becomes bow down) and frictional resistance is abruptly decreased as forward movement is abruptly accelerated.

(Ooching is only permitted to initiate surfing or planing.)

4.4 Ooching. Note attitude of boat—bow just beginning to drop—when ooching is effective.

Rapid Course Alteration

Frictional resistance is abruptly decreased as the rudder is angulated abruptly and the hull separates momentarily from the turbulent elements of its boundary layer.

UPWIND AND OFFWIND

Rocking

In addition to increasing and altering the direction of the apparent wind, rocking decreases the underwater (frictional) resistance by momentarily separating the hull from the turbulent elements of its boundary layer.

TECHNIQUES INTENDED TO CREATE A DRIVING FORCE—PROHIBITED BY RULE 54

SCULLING

Hydrodynamic lift, acting forward, results from rapid angulation of the rudder and its slow recovery to the mid-position.

Repetition of this action is prohibited.

PUMPING

Abrupt thrust of the sails aft results in a driving force acting forward (in excess of that acting aft in a slow recovery); that is, the "pump effect" can be used to create as well as increase aerodynamic force.

Repetition of this action is prohibited (except as indicated above).

OOCHING

Abrupt thrust of the body against a forward portion of the hull or rig results in a driving force acting forward (in excess of that acting aft in a slow recovery).

This action is prohibited except to initiate surfing or planing.

ROCKING (including "repeated vertical or athwartships body movement," persistent rolling, and repeated roll tacking and roll jibing)

Offwind rocking of eased sails through an athwartships arc results in aerodynamic lift acting forward, and rocking of the keel (or centerboard) and rudder (if they are appropriately shaped) results in hydrodynamic lift acting forward.

Repetition of this action is prohibited.

5

Gears

GO GEAR (ACCELERATION)

PROBLEMS

Slow acceleration after tacks, waves, gusts, or starting.

SOLUTION *(Fig. 5.1)*

Provide twist so that, despite disturbed air, pitching, rolling, and yawing, some portion of the sail (at the correct angle of incidence) will retain attached flow.

Increase draft so that increased twist will not diminish aerodynamic force.

Move draft forward in jib to facilitate attached flow at the leading edge and reduce side force.

Provide flexibility—a resilient rig that will adapt to abrupt changes in wind strength and direction.

Increase heading angle so that aerodynamic force is more aligned with heading.

INITIAL SETTINGS

Set mast bend at the minimum appropriate to the sail design.

Ease mainsheet and jibsheet to provide twist—all leech telltales flowing.

Sag jibstay by easing backstay (or shrouds), if possible.

Move jib lead forward, clew attachment aft, or jib up stay to increase fullness and close leech (despite twist).

Tension vang to provide flexibility—sag jibstay and float boom end.

Ease outhaul to provide fullness in lower sections.

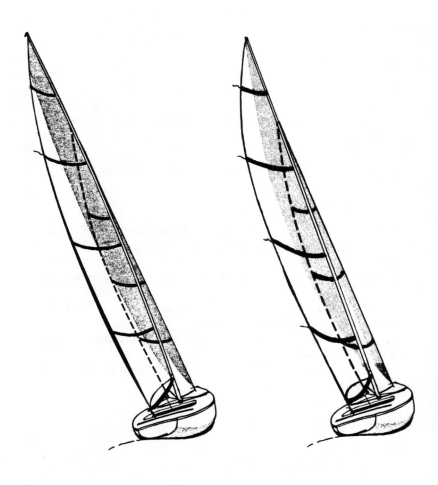

5.1. "Go gear." Note on boat to the right minimal mast bend, open leeches (with all leech telltales flowing), draft forward in jib, aft in main.

Tension jib luff or sag jibstay to provide a full leading edge and a flat leech.

Set jib lead position and main traveler in their most inboard positions (to facilitate twist).

Head lower.

ADJUSTMENTS AS THE BOAT GAINS SPEED

Reduce twist by tensioning main and jibsheet gradually.

Increase mast bend gradually.

Head higher.

Allow draft to move aft by easing jib luff, tensioning jibsheet, and reducing jibstay sag.

Move jib lead aft (or clew attachment forward or jib down stay).

In smooth water: increase sheeting angles as twist is eliminated; increase outhaul and reduce vang tension.

MINIMUM PRACTICABLE ADJUSTMENTS AS THE BOAT GAINS SPEED

Sheet in gradually and head up gradually.

Increase mast bend gradually (appropriate to speed); that is, in dinghies don't assume a full hike, in keel boats don't apply full backstay tension—until boat is up to speed.

LOW LEEWAY GEAR

PROBLEMS

Relatively low boat speed compared with wind speed (associated with very light or very heavy air), resulting in a high leeway angle or stalling of underwater surfaces.

Competitors, at same heading angle, moving to windward.

SOLUTION (Fig. 5.2)

Increase heading angle (align aerodynamic force with heading).

Increase sheeting angle (decrease side force and leeway angle and increase speed).

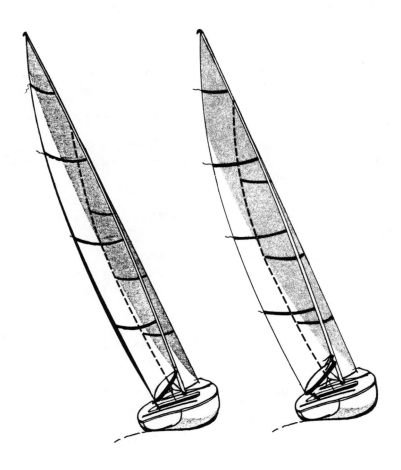

5.2. "Low leeway gear." Note on boat to the right leads outboard, flat sails with their draft forward.

Decrease draft (decrease aerodynamic force and side force).

Move draft forward (decrease side force).

Provide twist *if* (but only *if*) wind is highly variable in strength or direction, air is disturbed, and boat is pitching and/or yawing (common problems in very light or very heavy air).

INITIAL SETTINGS

Ease main traveler car and move jib lead to leeward.

Increase mast bend (decrease draft).

Hike "harder."

Tension outhaul and vang (reduce fullness in lower sections).

Tension jib luff and main Cunningham (provide a flat, low side force, low "drag" leech).

Head lower.

Ease mainsheet and jibsheet (if wind strength and/or direction is variable).

MINIMUM PRACTICABLE ADJUSTMENTS FOR SUDDEN INCREASE IN LEEWAY

Ease main traveler.

Hike "harder" and/or tension backstay.

Tension Cunningham.

Head lower.

RELATION TO "GO GEAR"

Low leeway gear is similar to "go gear" except that the sails are flatter, the leads are outboard, and twist is not necessarily used.

POINTING GEAR

PROBLEM

Movement to windward (pointing) is desired for the following reasons.

The boat has attained near maximum speed in moderate air, smooth water.

A boat on the leebow is disturbing the airflow or will force a tack. Just after the start, competitors in the front rank threaten to pass. A boat on the weather quarter must be stopped.

SOLUTION *(Fig. 5.3)*

Decrease both heading angle and sheeting angle.

Highest pointing is achieved when the boom is on the centerline, the jib leads are in their most inboard position, and the leeches of both

5.3. "Pointing gear." Note on boat to the left leads inboard, leeches closed, jibstay straight, upper mainsail leech telltales stalled.

sails are "closed" (i.e., the upper leeches are parallel to the centerline, the lower leeches are angled slightly inboard). These settings are appropriate in moderate air (4–12 knots) and smooth water (but only after the boat is up to speed). Then they result in both higher pointing and an increase in speed made good to windward (V_{mg}).

Pointing is not related to windward yawing moment (weather helm) whether due to imbalance of power in sails, heeling, rake, or any other factor. Additional rudder angulation has no advantageous effect upon pointing. However, a slight weather yawing moment does cause the boat to head up whenever the helmsman's attention lapses and therefore contributes to gains to windward.

PURPOSE

Pointing gear may only be used to achieve optimal performance in moderate air and smooth water. (In light air and in waves, speed, rather than high pointing, produces optimal V_{mg}, and in heavy air reduction in leeway and heeling are more important). However, for brief periods, pointing gear is also appropriate for situations in which a move to windward is more important than optimal performance.

INITIAL SETTINGS

Increase mast bend so as to decrease draft in both main and jib (to prevent an increase in side force as sheeting angle is decreased) in winds above the design wind; decrease mast bend in winds below the design wind.

Decrease sheeting angles (reduce "drag angle") by moving main traveler car and jib leads inboard.

Increase mainsheet and jibsheet tensions (decrease twist), thereby causing all sections of both sails to operate at reduced sheeting angles —upper leech telltales should be just stalled.

Head higher.

Allow draft to remain aft (horizontal wrinkles along the luffs of both sails) where increased mast bend and sheet tension move it.

Set a jib (if choice exists) with a flat entry.

Control jibstay sag (through mast bend modifications) to match the jib luff curve. (Do not allow excess sag to move draft forward, make leading edge full, and require an increase in heading angle.)

PRACTICABLE ADJUSTMENTS TO INCREASE POINTING RAPIDLY

Increase mast bend (increase backstay or vang tension) in winds above the design wind; decrease mast bend (decrease backstay or vang tension) in winds below the design wind.

Move main traveler car and jib lead to most inboard positions.

Tension mainsheet and jibsheet to close leeches.

Head higher.

STARTING GEAR

PROBLEMS

The presence of disturbed air and water and other boats which interfere with access to the preferred position on the line, in clear air, and on time.

The need to accelerate rapidly in the midst of disturbed air and water.

After the gun the need to point high, despite disturbed air and water, so as to separate from the fleet and the headed air within it.

SOLUTION

During the Approach

Know the location of the line
Be on time
Come up close under the weather boat
Maintain a windward yawing moment
Point, don't foot

Just Prior to the Start

Accelerate rapidly

After the Gun

Shift from "Go Gear" to "Pointing Gear" as soon as the boat is up to speed

INITIAL SETTINGS

"Go Gear" *(Fig. 5.4)*

Set mast bend at the minimum appropriate to the sails

Ease mainsheet and jibsheet to provide sufficient twist—both sails luffing moderately

> Use mark on sheet to determine (approximate) approach setting

> Use additional mark for subsequent acceleration setting

Tension vang to provide flexibility and to assure that the main produces more power than the jib—that is, to maintain windward yawing moment

Jib luff should be full due to jibstay sag but Cunningham should be eased

Set jib lead position and main traveler car in their most inboard positions

Head High

Close up under boats to windward (high speed not required until moment of acceleration)

ACCELERATION SETTINGS (Fig. 5.4)

"Go Gear—Plus"

Trim mainsheet until luffing ceases but leech telltales are still flowing

Trim jibsheet (synchronously) until luffing ceases but all telltales are flowing; keep jib open, moderately twisted

Head Down to Close-Hauled—but not below close-hauled, if avoidable

AFTER THE GUN SETTINGS

"Pointing Gear"—As the Boat Gains Speed

Increase mast bend *gradually* (if wind velocity is less than 4 or greater than 12 knots)

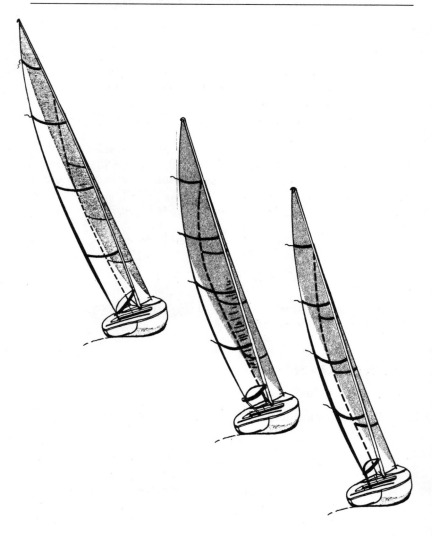

5.4. "Starting gear"—initial and acceleration settings. Note on boat in the middle minimal mast bend, leads inboard, open, twisted leeches, jibstay sagged, all leech telltales flowing (initial setting). Note on boat to the right increased leech tension in both main and jib (but all leech telltales still flowing) (acceleration setting).

Decrease twist by tensioning main and jibsheet *gradually* until
  leeches are "closed" with upper leech telltales stalled
Allow draft to move aft by tensioning jibstay (or easing jib luff)
  and by increasing mast bend
Keep boom on centerline, jib lead in maximum inboard position
Reduce vang tension in smooth water
Increase outhaul tension (if wind velocity is less than 4 or greater
  than 12 knots) particularly in smooth water

Head Higher

Do not attempt "Pointing Gear" or attempt it only partially in:

Very light air
Very heavy air
Waves

RECOVERY

Once out on the course in clear air, separated from the fleet, shift
to whatever sail trim is appropriate to the wind velocity and the
waves.

6
Special Considerations: Upwind

YAWING BALANCE

PROBLEM

Negation of a yawing moment requires either that the CE, through alterations in mast position or sail trim (or both), or the CLR, through movement of the centerboard or rudder or through altered angulation of the rudder, be shifted. The rudder should be used as little as possible to counteract yawing moments; changing its position to a less efficient angle results in excess drag for the hydrodynamic lift created. A boat which, in a particular condition and with its rudder within the range of optimal angulation, has no or very little yawing moment is said to be well "balanced"; one in which a significant mal-alignment of the forces and an arm "*a*" exist and in which nonoptimal rudder angulation is required is said to be poorly "balanced."

The rudder, because it operates in the denser medium, water, because it can be angulated independently of the hull, and because it (sometimes) is a pure foil with no mast or keel ahead of it, is very efficient. Increasing the angle of incidence, the leeway angle, of a foil, as the resultant force is directed more forward, is more efficient than increasing the speed of the overlying flow. This phenomenon is particularly useful to the rudder, which, in contrast with the keel or centerboard, may operate at an increased angle of incidence without increasing the leeway angle of the whole boat and without increasing the resistance of the hull (as happens when the hull "crabs" through the water at a high leeway angle). Because of its efficiency (the production of a large laterally acting force with very little drag) and because of the wide range of its efficiency, the rudder is characteristically used as the primary adjuster of balance. Even the "fine touch" on the tiller is associated with almost continuous minor manipulations. This and even greater movements are acceptable because of the rudder's basic efficiency and because it is the only available means of simultaneously modifying the total hydrodynamic force produced, the direction of that force, and, by displacing the CLR, the alignment of that force. However, when the angulation required to achieve these effects is outside the optimal range (a "weather helm" or a "lee helm"), that is, when the sail or hull trim is inappropriate, modifications of "balance" are in order.

SOLUTION

Achieve balance while maintaining rudder angulation within the optimal range by:

Shifting the center of lateral resistance:
Moving centerboard position
Moving rudder position
Moving crew weight (or other ballast)
Shifting the center of effort:
Moving the mast position

Test balance by setting sails in optimal trim for the conditions. If the rudder cannot be maintained at an optimal angulation and/or if performance is defective, further movement of the centerboard, rudder, ballast, or mast should be tested.

Set rake for optimal sail trim and optimal performance, not primarily to achieve balance. Maximum rake is desirable to windward to improve speed, particularly in high-speed (moderate air and smooth water) conditions. (Neither rake nor windward yawing moment is essential to pointing.)

RESPONSES (PRACTICAL)

Achieve balance for most sailing conditions by changing or moving centerboard, rudder, or mast.

A rig that is balanced in moderate air usually has a leeward yawing moment in light air and a windward yawing moment in heavy air.

In light air the leeward yawing moment can be reduced by *(Fig. 6.1A):*

Increased rake: shifting center of effort aft
Heeling: shifting crew weight to leeward
Depressing the bow: shifting crew weight forward
Increased fullness in the main (only acceptable after speed has
    been developed)

In heavy air the windward yawing moment can be reduced by *(Fig. 6.1B):*

Decreased rake: shifting center of effort forward
Decreased heeling: reducing shift to leeward of center of effort
    through decreased draft, increased twist, increased sheeting
    angle, reduced heading angle, or increased hiking
An appropriate gust response: acceleration rather than heeling
Careful steering to prevent heeling in gusts and waves and to
    recover speed thereafter
Depressing the stern: shifting crew weight aft

DIRTY AIR

CIRCUMSTANCES (IN LIGHT TO MODERATE AIR)

In the midst of the fleet
    At the start
    Approaching the weather mark
Within the backwind or blanket zone of another boat or boats
Within zones of erratic airflow
    Near windward or leeward barriers (confined waters)
    Within inversions (warm air layered over cold) which are
        breaking up or developing: vertical air mixing
    Within zones of convergence: horizontal air mixing
In waves

PROBLEM

To prevent stalling and to minimize drag (i.e., retain attached flow
over entire sail surface) despite rapid and repeated changes in the
velocity and angle of incidence of the airflow (or in the position of the
sails).

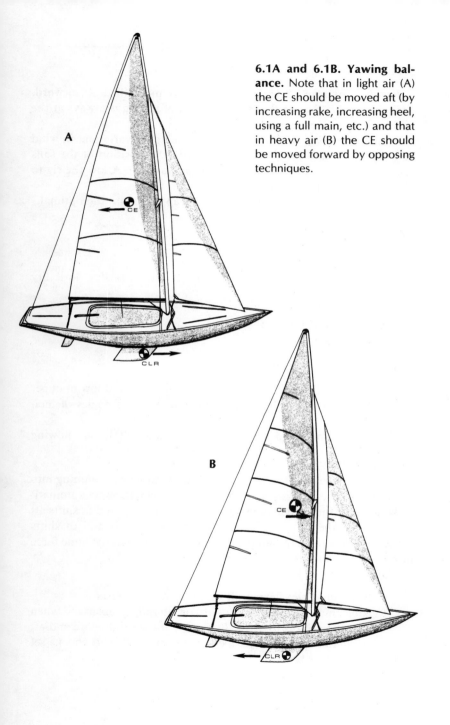

6.1A and 6.1B. Yawing balance. Note that in light air (A) the CE should be moved aft (by increasing rake, increasing heel, using a full main, etc.) and that in heavy air (B) the CE should be moved forward by opposing techniques.

SOLUTIONS (Fig. 6.2)

Facilitate attached flow: Increase fullness and shift draft forward.

Provide twist: Ensure that some portion of the rig is always at the optimal angle of incidence.

Provide flexibility: Ensure that the sails adapt to variations in wind velocity (gusts and lulls) and variations in the position of the sails relative to the wind (pitching, rolling, and yawing). Allow the rig to "breathe"; "ventilate" the rig.

Adjust sail trim continuously: So as to approximate the optimal.

RESPONSES

Keep Sails Full

> Sag mast laterally: make mainsail full without losing flexibility of mast
> Sag jibstay
> Move jib lead forward
> Ease outhaul

Keep Leeches Twisted

> Keep angle of incidence high in lower sections and low in upper sections (achieve maximum possible range of angles of incidence)
> Ease mainsheet and jibsheet until all leech telltales are flowing

Make Rig Flexible

Arrange for sails to flex in gusts and lulls and when slamming into waves (instead of jerking and emptying). Permit them to automatically decrease their angle of incidence (open) in gusts and in shifts aft and increase their angle of incidence (close) in lulls and in shifts forward. Allow them to pump so as to increase the aerodynamic force in recovery from gusts.

Mainsail flexibility is provided by:

> Flexible mast tip: flexing aft or to leeward in gusts
> Flexible mid-mast: flexing forward or laterally in gusts and when slamming into waves; facilitated by initial bend—fore and aft or lateral; spreaders, jumpers, lower shrouds, and chocks set to facilitate bend

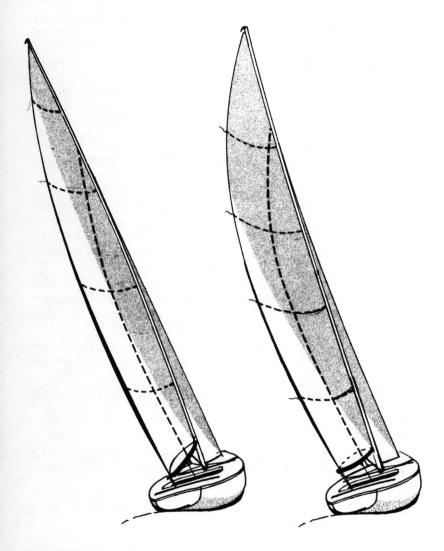

6.2. Dirty air trim. Note on the boat to the right full sails, open, twisted leeches, vang control of boom, lateral mast sag, jibstay sag, and all leech telltales flowing.

Increased rake: inefficient angle of attachment of jibstay permits more movement of mast tip

Flexible boom end: vang control (instead of mainsheet) provides an inefficient angle of attachment which permits more movement of boom end; eased mainsheet permits boom to lift (against vang) in gust

"Flexible" mainsail: flat leech with draft forward permits the leech to open in gust

Jib flexibility is provided by:

Flexible jibstay: initial sag should be provided by bending the mid-mast through vang tension, chocking, or shroud/spreader relationships.

Sag aft makes the jib fuller and moves the draft forward, sag to leeward makes the jib fuller and shifts the draft aft—*if the leech stays in the same position.* However, in boats whose jib heads are attached by long pennants (at a significant distance from the mast), as the stay sags the leech moves aft and to leeward so that the leech is twisted open.

The important net effect of a sagging jibstay in dirty air in most boats (with fractional rigs) is that the jib is made more adaptable to gusts and waves, the leech is twisted open, and the draft is shifted forward.

Flexible head and tack attachments: long pennants (halyard, tack downhaul) ease (rather than jerk) the head and tack in gusts and slams.

Flexible clew attachment: eased jibsheet (not two-blocked) eases the clew in gusts and slams.

Modify Trim Rapidly

Provide immediate modification of mainsheet, jibsheet, and luff tension in response to variations in wind velocity and direction.

WAVES

PROBLEM

Maintain maximum speed (V_{mg}) despite abrupt changes in forward progress, pitching, yawing, and rig movement (which cause dramatic changes in angle of incidence—stalling and luffing), decreased driving

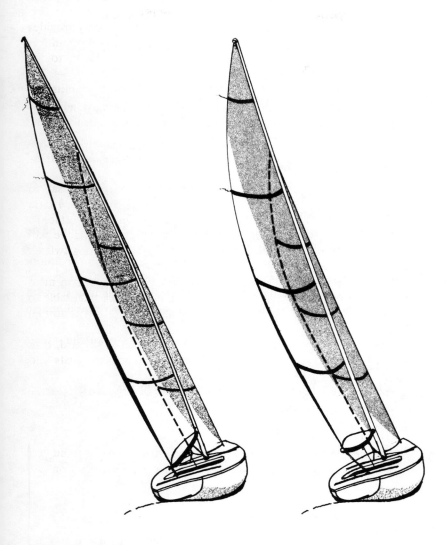

6.3. Wave trim. Note on the boat to the right fullness and twist (both sails), lateral mast sag, jibstay sag, forward position of draft in jib, and inboard lead positions.

force, increased resistance, and increased leeway. Respond to each wave as it appears so as to diminish its adverse effect.

SOLUTION *(Fig. 6.3)*

Basic Trim Changes

Increase fullness in both main and jib, shift draft forward in jib, and twist sails so as to increase aerodynamic force, decrease side force, and decrease leeway.

Pitch Responsiveness

Use vang tension to provide rig flexibility.

Appropriate Sails and Rig

Jib: Full jib with draft forward (large luff curve to accommodate significant jibstay sag), flat leech, and flat head.

Main: Low luff curve main with full lower sections (to accommodate increased vang tension), flat leech, and flat head. (Flat leeches and flat heads open readily, that is, are less likely to stall, in gusts, with impacts, and with large variations in angle of incidence and diminish pitching and rolling.)

Mast: Flexible tip to increase mainsail tolerance of pitching.

Stability

Minimize pitching, rolling, and yawing moments.

BASIC TRIM

Twist Sails

Ease mainsheet
Ease jibsheet

Increase Aerodynamic Force

Increase draft in mainsail by straightening mast (fore and aft) creating lateral mid-mast sag, and easing outhaul.

Increase draft in jib by sagging jibstay and easing sheet and by keeping or moving jib lead forward.

Decrease Side Force

Increase sheeting angles through twist (keep traveler car and jib lead inboard to increase range of twist)

Increase heading angle: head lower (tolerated without an increase in side force because leeches are open)

Decrease Leeway

Decrease side force through twist and increased sheeting angles

Increase speed through increased driving force and increased heading angle, thereby generating greater hydrodynamic lift force from underwater fins

Shift Draft Forward in Jib

Tension jib luff and increase jibstay sag so as to facilitate attached flow at leading edge despite pitching and yawing

Maintain Constant Angle of Heel

Find a "groove," an angle of heel, that permits the boat to be steered without significant yawing and with the least possible pitching and rolling *(Fig. 6.4)*

6.4. Rolling. The major changes in apparent wind direction induced by rolling cause alternate luffing and stalling and a marked reduction in the aerodynamic force produced.

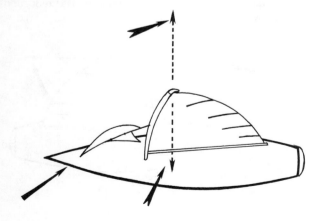

Primary Controls

Jibstay sag and main and jib sheet tension are the primary controls for waves and should be modified whenever a significant change in wave action occurs.

PITCH RESPONSIVENESS (Fig. 6.5)

Impact associated with pitching results (as the jibstay sag increases) in the jib leech opening (increasing twist and shifting draft forward) and (as the mast tip momentum stretches the leech) the main leech closing (decreasing twist and shifting draft aft). In recovery, the reverse occurs.

Recovery results (as the jibstay tenses) in the jib leech closing (decreasing twist and shifting draft aft) and (as the mast springs aft) in the main leech opening (increasing twist and shifting draft forward).

The sails must be trimmed so that for the greatest possible amount of time, despite pitching, they are full, that is, curving appropriately to leeward, and so that, short of emptying, they resist stalling. This character is called flexibility and is best provided by a fully battened sail set on a moderately flexible mast with a moderate amount of jibstay sag and a boom under vang tension. The flexible rig cushions the impact of meeting a breaking wave and of pounding into a trough.

6.5. Pitching. The major changes in apparent wind direction induced by pitching cause alternate luffing and stalling and a marked reduction in the aerodynamic force produced.

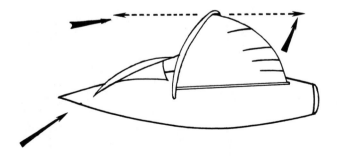

It prevents the sails from emptying so readily and diminishes the degree of leech closing associated with impacts. As the mast pitches forward, prior to impact, the apparent wind shifts forward. At impact in association with a lessened side force, the mainsail leech closes and, preventing the boat's bow from being blown down and over, the jib leech opens. As the mast pitches aft, in recovery (after impact and after slowing), the apparent wind shifts aft. Then, in association with an increased side force, the mainsail leech opens and, facilitating acceleration, the jib leech closes. A flexible top mast and flexible jibstay allow the rig to respond in this way but prevent over-response, jerking, and excessive disturbance of attached flow.

Vang tension is the chief determinant of pitch responsiveness as it limits (through jibstay sag) the jib leech closing in recovery from impact and limits (by facilitating elevation of the boom) the main leech closing in association with impact.

STABILITY

Minimize the Pitching Moment

Alter the period of free oscillation to make it disparate from that of wave-induced oscillation—usually (but not necessarily) achieved by keeping the crew, the gear, the mast, etc., close to the middle of the boat ("lighten the ends") and by keeping the weight of the mast low and the weight of the keel high.

Sail at a different angle to the waves or with the boat at a different angle of heel to alter the period of wave-induced oscillation.

Alter sail trim so that the upper sections, which describe the greatest arc, are not developing a driving force in both directions along the axis of the pitch. This is usually achieved by twisting the mainsail (and jib, if masthead) so that its upper leech is open on the pitch aft. The maneuver effectively applies a brake to the pitch during the reverse phase of every oscillation.

Minimize the Rolling Moment

Alter the period of free oscillation—usually (but not necessarily) achieved by keeping the crew spread apart (on opposite rails when sailing downwind) and standing up (particularly important in a single-handed dinghy where the crew cannot be "spread apart").

Sail at a different angle to the waves or at a different angle of heel. Alter sail trim so that the upper sections of the mainsail are flat and stalled in one phase of the roll and the upper sections of the spinnaker are flat and restricted from additional oscillation. This is usually achieved by vanging the mainsail and trimming the boom more inboard (less in line with the axis of roll) and by using a spinnaker with flat upper sections (avoiding rounded edges), a fully hoisted halyard, and an over-trimmed sheet and guy.

Minimize the Yawing Moment

Alter the period of free oscillation—difficult, but may be achieved by redistributing the crew, repositioning the mast, altering the relative power in main and jib, and/or, most effectively, by altering the design, size, and position of the rudder and keel or centerboard.

Steer carefully so as to keep the boat "on track" despite its tendency to yaw (very difficult in some boats). This is usually achieved by good "helmsmanship," an ability to concentrate on steering, achieved either by arranging for crew members to assume all other responsibilities or by arranging for gear to be adjusted without looking at it. (The prime characteristic of a good helmsman is his ability to sail his boat stably—with minimal pitching, rolling, or yawing.)

Alter sail trim so as to provide a range between luffing and stalling that is consistent with the helmsman's ability to steer. This is usually achieved by increasing twist (easing sheets) in proportion to the degree of instability. Leeches are tensioned and the boat is steered (with minimal pitching, rolling, or yawing) within a very narrow range in smooth water, and leeches are twisted and the boat is steered within a very wide range in waves.

RESPONSE TECHNIQUES

Decrease Slowing, Heeling, and Leeway in Wave Crest

IMMEDIATE RESPONSE

Head up: Head more directly into crest so as to decrease time spent in downwind moving water; decrease leeway from impact with crest; and decrease heeling due to elevation in crest.

Hike harder: Erect rig rapidly so as to shift apparent wind aft, permitting boat to be headed up without losing attached flow.

RECOVERY

After responding to wave crest:

Head down—bear off in trough
Ease mainsheet (and jibsheet if readily adjustable)
Maintain hike if necessary to prevent excessive heeling

Return to basic trim:

Head up to original angle
Diminish hike to allow moderate heel before hiking in next wave crest
Tension mainsheet (and jibsheet if eased) to basic position

Repeat with successive waves

GUST CONTROL

PROBLEM

Maintain maximum speed or permit acceleration despite a sudden increase in wind velocity, angle of incidence (the apparent wind shifts aft), total aerodynamic force, side force, heeling force, and yawing moment, associated with an increase in and shifting aft of draft in both the main and jib.

SOLUTION *(Fig. 6.6)*

Basic Trim Changes

Reduce aerodynamic force (and particularly side force and heeling force): twist leeches, reduce angle of incidence, decrease draft, and shift draft forward in both the main and jib. Eliminate leeward yawing moment (if present).

Gust Responsiveness

Provide a flexible topmast, bending aft and to leeward, and a flexible boom controlled by the vang rather than the mainsheet. Provide flat leeches that will open in the gust (rig flexibility).

Appropriate Sails and Rig

Jib: flat in smooth water, fuller in waves, with a flat leech and a flat, open head

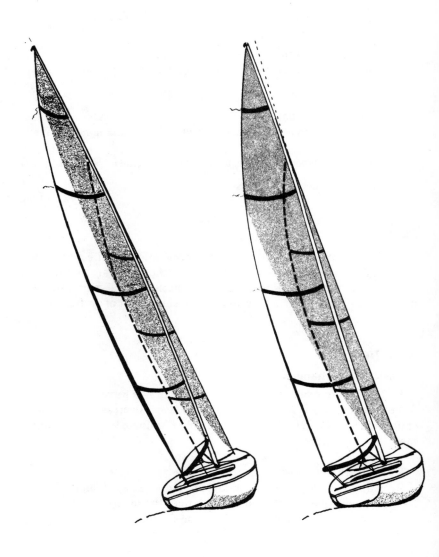

6.6 Gust control. Note on boat to the right flatness, twist, and forward position of draft in both sails, flat leeches, and outboard lead position.

Main: large luff curve in smooth water, small luff curve in waves, with a flat leech and a flat, open head
Mast: flexible tip that will bend aft and laterally in gust

BASIC TRIM AND GUST RESPONSIVENESS

Provide Twist and Gust Responsiveness

Ease mainsheet and jibsheet, and/or tension backstay.

Tension vang (while easing the mainsheet). Permit the boom to lift more readily in a gust; cause the lower main, where the greatest power and fullness lie, to be flattened and the leech to twist. Cause the jib leech to open and its draft to shift forward.

Shift Draft (and Direction of Aerodynamic Force) Forward

Tension Cunningham (as the vang and/or backstay bend the mast). Keep the draft forward and prevent the leech from closing.

Tension jib tack downhaul (if available) or halyard (if practicable) to make the leading edge full and the leech flat.

Decrease Leeward Yawing Moment

Flatten and twist jib (as above) and reduce its angle of incidence (shift its lead outboard) sufficiently so that the combined center of effort shifts aft.

Move crew weight forward and (in centerboarders) move the centerboard forward—shift the center of lateral resistance forward.

Boat should head up automatically (and heel but minimally), not be blown down and over, as a gust hits.

RESPONSE TECHNIQUES

Smooth Water (Practicable Response as Gust Hits)

Decrease angle of incidence through a combination of decreased heading angle and increased sheeting angle—because the boat is going fast, is easy to steer, and is making little leeway.

Head up and drop the main traveler!

Distance traveler is dropped, must be tested until gain to windward in the gust can be achieved without either deceleration or increased leeway; if deceleration and heeling are occurring, despite large drop, the upper main may need more initial twist.

If feasible (jib on traveler), shift jib lead outboard simultaneously.

Waves (Practicable Response as Gust Hits)

Both sails should be well twisted and the vang should "float" the boom (basic trim).

Because the boat is moving slowly, is making leeway, is difficult to steer, and cannot be headed up without further loss of speed, the aerodynamic force, side force, and heeling force should be decreased as the gust hits by *easing the mainsheet, tensioning the backstay, or tensioning the vang.*

In most small centerboard boats, easing the mainsheet should be the initial response to a gust (though not in boats such as Lasers in which mast flexibility opens the leech sufficiently). In boats such as FD's and 5-0-5's, whose masts are made flexible by vang tension (driving the lower mast to windward and the mast tip to leeward), tensioning the vang opens the leech and is the preferred initial response. In racing keelboats dropping the traveler is usually the best initial response (tensioning the backstay may be preferable in waves).

Basic twist and leech flexibility permit acceleration in small gusts without alteration in heading or sheeting angles. The degree of twist should be increased until acceleration rather than slowing is produced by such gusts.

Recovery

After responding to gust:

> Head down
> Ease mainsheet (or tension backstay) and ease jibsheet and/or jib traveler (if not already so modified); hike harder

Return to basic trim:

> Head up to original angle
> Return traveler to original position
> Tension mainsheet, tension jibsheet, and ease backstay to basic positions (if altered)

LIGHT AIR
Stage I: High Viscosity Flow Regime
Beginning Driving Force, Absent Hydrodynamic Side Force
Apparent wind velocity: 0–2 knots
Primary concerns: power, leeway, and balance

Initiation of forward movement: requires a wide sheeting angle and a wide heading angle

Excess leeway: requires flat sails with draft forward

Yawing imbalance: requires heeling and an open, twisted jib

Stage II: Laminar Separation Regime
Maximum Driving Force Sought but Unattainable

Apparent wind velocity: 2–4 knots

Primary concerns: power and pointing

Speed (insufficient): requires power—full sails and a wide heading angle

Pointing: requires progressively more narrow sheeting and heading angles as speed increases

PROBLEMS

Maintain speed and minimize leeway despite minimal aerodynamic force and minimal hydrodynamic lift force (low speed and high leeway angle), defective sail shape, variable apparent wind direction, and leeward yawing moment.

SOLUTIONS

Use maximum rake to counteract the leeward yawing moment (typical of most boats in light air).

Use a pre-bent mast (if necessary) to obtain jibstay sag appropriate to the jib luff curve and mast bend appropriate to the mainsail luff curve.

Increase speed and decrease leeway through a combination of trim appropriate to:

Go gear

Low leeway gear

Maintain constant, convex-to-leeward sail shape despite sagging sail cloth and collapse of shape during leeward rolling.

Provide twist (lower airflow is slowed by friction: apparent wind aloft is further aft).

Provide balance: increase weather yawing moment.

Separate jib leech and leeward surface of main (open "slot") particularly in very light air (when flow is viscous and resists moving between sails).

RESPONSES (THEORETICAL)

Initiate forward motion in low leeway gear:

Increase sheeting angles
Open leeches to provide twist
Use flat sails

When forward motion is sustained, shift to "go gear":

Decrease sheeting angles
Close leeches (partially)
Make sails fuller—shift draft forward in jib, aft in main

Seek speed, ignore pointing.
Heel boat to leeward to maintain sail shape (despite rolling).
Shift crew weight forward and to leeward to increase weather yawing moment.
Head down: head higher gradually, if speed is sustained. Avoid oversteering, that is, avoid course changes for slight variations in wind direction (retrim sails instead).

RESPONSES (PRACTICAL)

Use full jib, flat main.
When initiating forward motion (1–2 knots) (high viscosity flow regime) *(Fig. 6.7):*

Ease travelers: shift jib leads outboard, boom off centerline
Increase twist: lift jib clew by hand—elevate boom with topping
    lift, spinnaker halyard, or by hand
Flatten sails:
    Bend mast (through "pre-bend" preferably)
    Tension outhaul
Sag jibstay (through "pre-bend preferably)
Separate jib leech from mainsail (open "slot")
Trim hull: heeled, bow down
Head down
Keep the jib luff telltales just short of stalling and, at the same
    time, the main leech telltales flowing freely

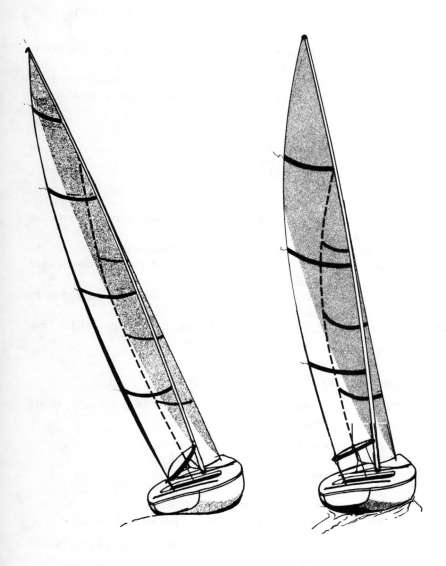

6.7. Very light air trim. Note on boat to the right full jib, flat main, increased mast bend and twist, leads displaced outboard, and open slot.

When forward motion is sustained (3–6 knots) (laminar separation regime) *(Fig. 6.8):*

Shift travelers up: shift jib leads gradually more inboard, boom toward centerline

Reduce twist: tension vang (mainsheet used as traveler control) until upper leech approaches a parallel-to-boom position

Sag jibstay through vang tension:
Shift draft forward
Make jib fuller and more flexible

Make sails fuller:
Reduce mast bend toward optimal
Ease outhaul

Allow draft to move aft:
Counteract jibstay sag by easing luff (till horizontal wrinkles appear)
Ease Cunningham (til horizontal wrinkles appear)

Head: gradually higher—speed rather than pointing sought until maximum speed achieved

Heel boat and hold boom whenever rolling imminent so as to preserve sail shape

Trim hull optimally without heeling and without undue bow immersion as soon as boat is "up to speed"

RESPONSE TO VELOCITY VARIATIONS

"Power down" just before entering lull (less than 3 knots), hitting wave, reaching disturbed air:

Ease mainsheet and jibsheet: increase twist
Increase mast bend: straighten lateral sag
Ease vang (if used)
Head down
Shift crew weight to leeward and forward
Tension outhaul and jib halyard (if problem sustained)

"Power up" after entering gust (less than 3 knots), finding smooth water, reaching clear air:

Tension mainsheet and jibsheet
Decrease mast bend: increase lateral sag

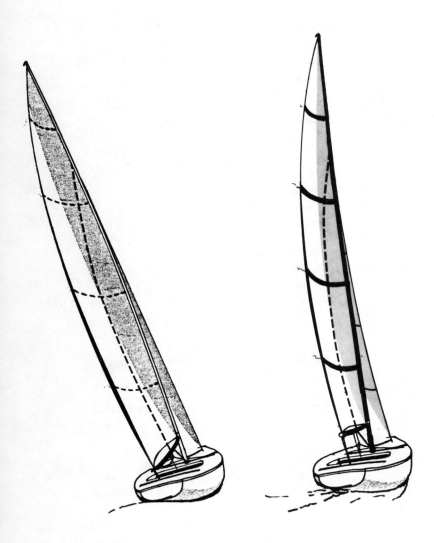

6.8. Light air trim. Note on boat to the right less twist, leads more inboard, straighter mast (lateral sag), fuller mainsail, draft farther aft, in comparison to "very light air trim," plus marked jibstay sag.

Tension vang (if used)
Hold course and then head up
Shift crew weight to windward and aft
Ease outhaul and jib halyard (if advantage sustained)

RESPONSE TO WAVES

"Power up" for waves (dying wind, many boats, etc.):

Make rig flexible:
Shift leech control from mainsheet to vang
Make sails fuller:
Tension vang: sag jibstay
Decrease mast bend
Ease outhaul
Ease Cunningham and ease jib luff (to counteract shift of draft
forward with jibstay sag)
But increase twist:
Travelers up: jib leads inboard, boom on centerline
Ease mainsheet and jibsheet
And head down

MODERATE AIR
Stage III: Turbulent Attached Flow Regime
Maximum Heeling Force without Heeling
Apparent wind velocity: 4–8 knots
Primary concerns: pointing and power (insufficient)
Pointing: requires narrowest possible sheeting and heading
angles
Speed: requires power

Stages IV–V: Design Wind Regime
*Additional Heeling Force and Driving Force with Moderate, Controlled
Heeling*
Apparent wind velocity: 8–14 knots
Primary concerns: power (excessive) *and pointing*
Heeling: requires flatter sails and maximum righting moment
(hiking)
Pointing: requires narrowest possible sheeting and heading
angles

PROBLEMS

Utilize optimal sailing conditions (high speed and minimal leeway) to achieve best possible combination of pointing and speed (4–8 knots) and best pointing (8–12 knots).

SOLUTIONS *(Fig. 6.9)*

Point high and maintain maximum speed through a combination of trim appropriate to:

Pointing gear
Go gear

Close leeches and reduce sheeting angles to produce minimum possible drag angle. Leading edge should split the approaching airflow and leeches should be on the centerline (to produce maximum deviation of the airflow and highest possible pointing).

RESPONSES (THEORETICAL)

As speed is acquired, shift from "go gear" toward pointing gear:

Decrease sheeting angles
Close leeches
Shift draft aft

Retain elements of go gear:

Full sails

Seek pointing even at a slight reduction in speed.
Keep boat bolt upright (or on optimal lines).
Hull trim: optimal to facilitate (approximately) 4° windward rudder angulation.
Head up: utilize every increase in wind strength to head higher (as apparent wind shifts aft).

RESPONSES (PRACTICAL)

Use full jib, full main.
As speed is acquired:

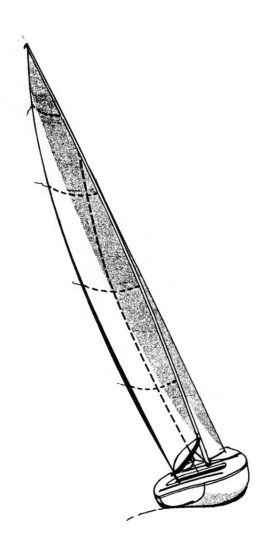

6.9. Moderate air trim. "Standard boat"—note closed leeches (upper tell-tales stalled), leads inboard, sails full, mast straight (laterally and fore and aft), draft aft, straight jibstay.

Shift leads to most inboard positions, boom on centerline
Decrease mast bend
Tension mainsheet and jibsheet to bring leeches into maximally
closed positions: upper leech telltales just stalling (mast stiff-
ness must be sufficient to allow this)
Release vang: control main with mainsheet
Reduce jibstay sag to that which is appropriate to the designed
jib luff curve
Ease cunningham and jib luff to keep draft 50 percent aft
Ease outhaul until vertical wrinkles appear
Sag mast laterally (if necessary) to provide optimal mainsail
fullness and appropriate jibstay sag

Head up until boat begins to slow and windward telltales on jib lift
continuously.

Hike as "hard" as possible to keep boat bolt upright with crew
weight distributed for optimal hull immersion.

RESPONSE TO VELOCITY VARIATIONS

Vary course with every variation in wind strength and direction:

Shoot up in gusts and then gradually fall away to original course
Steer to every variation in wind direction: keep windward telltale
of jib lifting

*"Power down" after initial response to velocity increase (12+ knots)
(See "Gust Response"):*

Tension Cunningham
Tension vang
Increase mast bend
Tension mainsheet and jibsheet (so that upper leech telltales are
just stalling)
Tension jib halyard (if horizontal luff wrinkles appear)

*"Power up" before entering lull (wind 8–12 knots, decreasing to
below 8 knots):*

Ease Cunningham
Ease vang
Decrease mast bend

Ease mainsheet and jibsheet (so that upper leech telltales are just stalling)

(Note that in moderate air "power down," "power up" responses are the reverse of light air when "power down" is appropriate to a lull and "power up" to a gust; that is, maximum power is appropriate to 8–12 knots and must be reduced either side of that wind strength)

HEAVY AIR

Stages VI–VII

Maximum Driving Force and Boat Speed to Windward

Apparent wind velocity: 14–30 knots

Primary concerns: power, leeway, balance, and adaptability

Heeling: requires flat sails (depth of chord approximately 5 percent) and increased sheeting angles

Leeway: requires flat sails (particularly aloft), increased sheeting angles, twist, and draft forward

Yawing imbalance: requires control of heeling and a flattened, twisted, and widely sheeted mainsail

Waves and gusts: require an adaptable, flexible rig

PROBLEMS

Maintain speed and minimal leeway and facilitate acceleration despite excess aerodynamic force, heeling, pitching, rolling, excess windward yawing moment, waves, gusts, and impaired steering.

SOLUTIONS (Fig. 6.10)

Reduce slowing and reduce leeway by a combination of trim appropriate to:

Low leeway gear
Go gear
Wave control
Gust control

Provide adaptability: a resilient rig that will adapt to abrupt changes in wind strength and direction.

Provide yawing balance to facilitate steering and acceleration.

Keep rig upright.

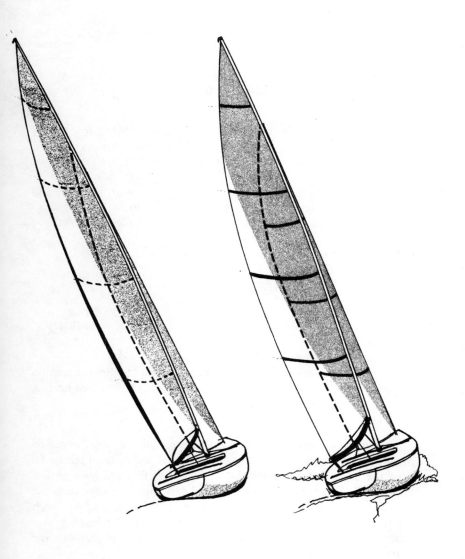

6.10. Heavy air trim. Note on boat to the right flat sails (increased mast bend), lateral mast bend (tip falloff), leads outboard, draft forward, vang tension, flat, open, twisted leeches.

RESPONSES (THEORETICAL)

Low leeway gear, go gear, and wave and gust control all require:

Twist
Increased sheeting angles (leads outboard)
Draft forward (particularly in jib)
Rig upright

Go gear and wave control require increased draft while low leeway gear and gust control require decreased draft; draft should, therefore, be a compromise and dependent upon whether the sea is rough or smooth.

Gust control requires heading up; low leeway gear, go gear, and wave control require heading down. The boat should be headed up with a gust and on the approach of a wave but headed off (lower) at all other times.

Head down: drive for speed.

Control gusts and waves:

1. In gusts or as wave approaches:
   Head up
   Ease mainsheet or traveler or tension vang or backstay
2. In recovery:
   Head down
   Ease mainsheet and jibsheet (and/or jib traveler) or tension backstay; hike "harder" (in presence of increased heeling force due to heading down)
3. Return to basic heading and trim

Jib should be designed for a large amount of jibstay sag (increased by strong winds and vang tension), twist, and a flat, open leech. To keep the leech flat, the draft should be pulled forward with jib luff tension. The lower part of the jib should be slightly flatter than the upper and the jibsheet should be tensioned so that the upper leech twists off approximately 10° and *opens in the gusts.* The leading edge should be full due to both jibstay sag and luff tension to facilitate the initiation of attached flow.

Main should be designed so that the upper leech is flat and will open in the gusts. The draft should be pulled forward with Cunningham tension. The lower mainsail should be full to accommodate the effects of the vang, but the lower leech should flatten with outhaul tension. The backstay-mainsheet-vang combination should provide both sufficient fullness and sufficient twist (upper batten off 5°–10°) so that the boat tolerates pitching, etc., but does not slow in gusts.

Balance requires a reduction in windward yawing moment by shifting lateral (underwater) resistance aft and aerodynamic force forward:

> Reduce power (draft and leech tension) in main
> Increase power in jib: full forward with a flat, twisted leech
> Decrease rake (in some boats)
> Keep rig upright

Rig upright requires reduced draft, twist, increased sheeting angles, decreased heading angle, and balance.

RESPONSES (PRACTICAL)

Decrease draft in main (particularly aloft) through increased backstay, vang, and/or chocking pressure.

Cause mast tip to "fall off" (bend aft and to leeward) in response to gust pressure on leech and movement of mid-mast forward and to windward (driven by shroud pressure on spreader, vang, or compression).

Shift travelers outboard (minimally in waves, maximally in smooth water).

Maintain draft in jib but shift it forward. Retain moderate air (fore and aft) jib lead position but increase luff tension.

Tension vang so as to make rig flexible and to facilitate gust and wave response.

Increase twist in main and jib (sufficient in main to minimize heeling and to retain slight windward yawing moment; sufficient in jib to prevent significant backwinding of main) but use sufficient mainsheet tension to keep mainsail from flogging.

Restore yawing balance (if necessary) by reducing rake. Maintain sufficient windward yawing moment (open jib leech) so that bow is not blown to leeward in gust.

Keep boat upright.

REDUCE SAIL AREA

When the aerodynamic side force cannot be reduced sufficiently by flattening the sails and reducing their angle of incidence (on boats where it is feasible), sail area should be reduced.

Reef the main: This is usually the initial technique as it improves yawing balance (decreases the weather yawing moment, "weather helm").

Change to a small jib: On boats using genoa jibs, a series of shorter-footed genoas (#2, #3, #4) and ultimately a nonoverlapping jib may be set as the wind velocity increases. The higher aspect ratio improves efficiency per unit of area (less drag, the aerodynamic force points more forward) and the shorter foot permits the sail to be sheeted both flatter and at a lower angle of incidence.

VERY HEAVY AIR

Stage VIII

Decreasing Boat Speed and Marked Leeway

Apparent wind velocity: 30+ knots

Primary concerns: speed, leeway, and balance

Speed (insufficient): requires increased heading and sheeting angles

Leeway: requires flat sails, increased sheeting angles, and draft forward

Yawing imbalance: requires balanced distribution of power and twist in main and jib

PROBLEMS

Prevent slowing and increased leeway due to abrupt variations in angle of incidence, balance, and sail shape associated with heeling, rocking, pitching, and yawing. Decrease resistance due to flogging, backwinding, and excess induced drag.

SOLUTIONS (Fig. 6.11)

Maintain steady (as much as possible) angle of heel, fore-and-aft trim, course, and sail shape. Keep rig flexible (jibstay and main leech) but do not allow sails to flog. Separate main and jib by trimming jib wide and open so as to avoid any backwinding of the main and so as to reduce induced drag (tip vortices) from the main.

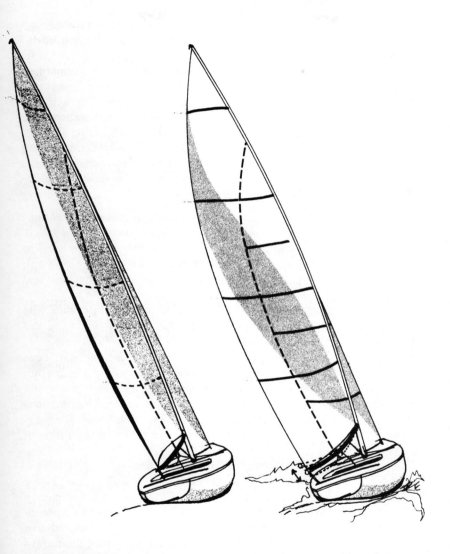

6.11. Very heavy air trim. Note on boat to the right increased lateral mast bend (tip falloff), leads maximally outboard, draft maximally forward, maximum vang tension (boom end flexible), and very flat, twisted leeches.

RESPONSES (THEORETICAL)

Provide twist, increased sheeting angles, and draft forward.

Provide flexibility (jibstay sag and boom end responsiveness) through vang tension.

Provide proportionate fullness in jib and main so as to maintain yawing balance and facilitate steering.

Steer carefully to maintain reasonably constant angle of incidence (course), angle of heel, and fore-and-aft trim (through appropriate wave management).

Trim jib more widely and with more twist than the main so as to prevent flogging, excessive backwinding, and excess induced drag.

RESPONSES (PRACTICAL)

Decrease draft in main (through mast bend and outhaul tension) until heeling, leeway, and windward yawing moment are controlled.

Arrange (by shroud adjustment) for mast tip to fall to leeward so as to decrease draft and move draft forward (particularly aloft), and cause lower mast to open to windward, thereby separating main and jib.

Provide twist in main proportionate to size of waves. Provide twist in jib so that jib leech matches leeward surface of main and produces no backwinding (or as little as possible).

Trim draft forward in main and jib so that leech becomes flat, locus of maximum fullness is less than 50 percent aft of luff, and backwind, if any, indents main evenly without flogging.

Apply sufficient vang tension to "float boom" (mainsheet functioning only to move boom laterally). Vang tension (with boom off centerline) pushes lower mast to windward and contributes to separation of main and jib.

Adjust jib lead (or traveler) well outboard and sheet jib so that bow is not blown to leeward nor is boat heeled in gusts, and so that yawing balance is preserved. Upper jib leech should open (be cut sufficiently flat so that it will open) as jibstay sags in gusts and upon hitting waves.

Tension mainsheet to just keep main leech from flogging.

Finally, distribute tension among mainsheet, vang, and main traveler so that boat does not have excess windward or leeward yawing moment, comes up into the wind easily, and accelerates (or at least does not slow) in gusts.

7

Special Conditions: Reaching

LIGHT AND MODERATE AIR REACHING

PROBLEMS

Maintain maximum speed while sailing the course (within 15° of the rhumb line) to attain clear air, the best possible sailing angle for the longest possible time, and the inside position (and the best possible sailing angle) on the approach to the next mark.

SOLUTIONS

Set the mainsail, spinnaker, and jib (if carried) to achieve the greatest possible aerodynamic force, while keeping the boat upright, in yawing balance, and with the least possible wetted surface. The greatest aerodynamic force is achieved when the sails are full (1:5 to 1:7 depth of chord ratio) and their angles of incidence are just short of stalling. Be prepared to alter sail trim so as to accommodate alterations in course to achieve the best strategic and tactical outcome.

RESPONSES—BASIC TRIM

Set the spinnaker for maximum power (maximum fullness with the draft 50 percent aft) at an angle of incidence just short of stalling *(Fig. 7.1)*.

Trim the spinnaker guy (pole) as far aft as possible so that the spinnaker's leading edge just splits the wind flow (begins to fold).

Ease the spinnaker sheet to keep the spinnaker luff collapsing (slightly) and so that the leeward telltales, over as large an area as possible, are flowing (the leech telltales must be expected to be stalled).

7.1. Aerodynamic force generated by the spinnaker. Note the distribution of aerodynamic lift and the importance of trimming the spinnaker as far to windward as possible.

7.2. Spinnaker sheet lead. Note the increase in driving force associated with trimming the sheet over the boom.

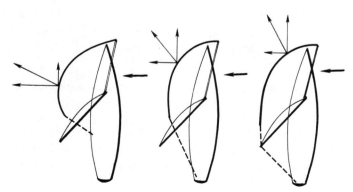

Lead the spinnaker sheet from the aftermost position on the boat and, in moderate air, from as high a position as possible, over the boom *(Fig. 7.2)*.

Keep the pole within 15° of horizontal (preferably horizontal) so as to hold the tack as far forward and outboard as possible.

Raise or lower the pole so as to keep the tack at approximately the same level as the clew. When close reaching, elevate the pole to the level to which the clew falls in the lulls—so that the luff will be full, the spinnaker shifted to windward by the lift of the full luff, and the leech open.

Keep the spinnaker halyard fully hoisted until (as the wind increases) the spinnaker head floats horizontally from the mast, then ease it (up to 12 inches, approximately). When, in stronger winds, the boat starts to heel, hoist it fully again so as to decrease the windward yawing moment (increased by the displacement of the spinnaker to leeward).

Set the mainsail for maximum power (maximum fullness with the draft 50 percent aft) at an angle of incidence just short of stalling (not just short of luffing as is done to windward).

Eliminate fore-and-aft mast bend and ease the Cunningham completely to allow the sail to become full and its draft to shift 50 percent aft.

Retain slight lateral mast bend, if necessary, to keep the draft from shifting forward excessively (with mast straightening).

Ease the traveler car fully and tension the vang to reduce mainsail twist.

Ease the mainsheet until all leech telltales are flowing (adjust the vang until all respond simultaneously), trim it in until they all stall, and then ease it until they just begin to flow. The sail is then generating the maximum possible aerodynamic force (with its leech just short of stalling).

Ease the outhaul until vertical wrinkles begin to appear along the foot.

Keep the boat in balance.

Keep the mast raked aft (as it was to windward) until, with increasing wind, weather helm and/or heeling develop. Then rake the mast forward.

Shift the crew weight forward to reduce wetted surface until, with increasing wind, weather helm and/or heeling develop. Then shift it aft.

Keep the boat upright by hiking as much as necessary, except to allow a slight heel in very light air. With increasing wind, allow the mainsail to twist and luff if necessary, to keep the boat upright. (The spinnaker supplies the majority of the driving force when reaching; the main supplies chiefly heeling force and windward yawing moment. It is far better to "rag" the main completely than to allow the boat to heel.)

Set the jib so as not to interfere with the spinnaker. Do not allow it to stall.

Ease the jibsheet as the boat bears away onto a reach. Ensure that, as the spinnaker is hoisted, the jib is not stalled. Keep all leeward (including leech) telltales flowing.

Ease the jib luff to allow the draft to move aft.

Displace the jib lead ("barber haulers," etc.) as far laterally as possible so as to reduce the angle of incidence without excessively increasing the fullness.

Displace the jib lead forward ("barber haulers," etc.) so as to reduce twist and keep the jib leech in conformity with the shape of the leeward surface of the main (to facilitate tangential flow from the jib leech onto the main).

Permit the jibstay to sag (by straightening the mast) but do not allow it to become so loose that the sail "pumps."

ADJUSTMENTS

Changes in Course, Wind Velocity, or Direction

No heading angle which allows the boat to sail within 15° of the rhumb line will increase the length of the leg significantly. Thus, for strategic and tactical purposes, a 30° variation (either side of the rhumb line) in sailing angle is acceptable. This variation in heading, combined with continual changes in wind velocity and direction, causes the angle of incidence to vary continuously while reaching. Sail trim, particularly while reaching, is never correct and, to approach the optimal for as much of the time as possible, should be continu-

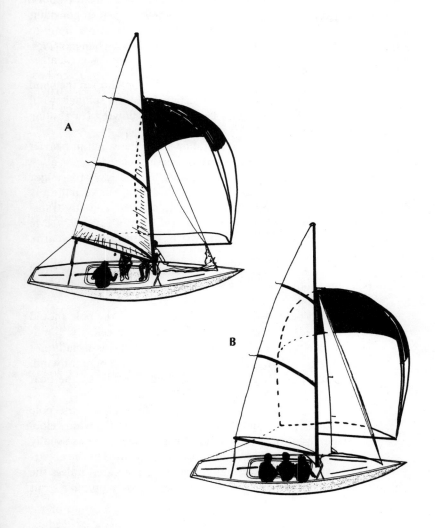

7.3A and 7.3B. Reaching trim—light and moderate air. Note spinnaker luff folding on left-hand boat, sheet led over boom, pole at same height as clew, pole horizontal in light air, but pole higher and farther aft on right-hand boat, halyard eased, jib hoisted, and leeches tighter in moderate air.

ously modified. Whereas to windward sail trim can be fixed (though twisted and flexible) and, to keep the angle of incidence near constant, the boat's heading can be continuously changed, while reaching, to achieve the same result, sail trim must be continuously changed *(Figs. 7.3A and 7.3B).*

Hold the spinnaker sheet and the mainsheet (or vang) in the hand and ease or trim them continuously to keep the spinnaker luff folding back and the main leech telltales flowing (or stalling intermittently).

In light air play the mainsheet, followed by the vang; in heavier air play the vang, followed by the mainsheet.

Change the spinnaker pole position (trim the guy) for major changes in course, wind velocity, or direction, but keep the guy cleated when its position is not being altered. The guy transmits the power of the spinnaker to the boat; if it is allowed to move the crew's arm, its power will be transmitted to that arm, not to the boat.

Except when the pole is set at its maximum height, its vertical position should be modified whenever (or immediately after) its horizontal position is changed.

As the boat bears away or the wind shifts aft, the pole should be lowered (and trimmed aft). As the wind velocity diminishes, the pole should also be lowered. (This is usually not associated with trimming the pole aft as the apparent wind, in a lull, initially shifts forward, and later, when the boat slows, it shifts but slightly aft.)

As the boat heads up or the wind shifts forward, the pole should be raised (and trimmed forward). As the wind velocity increases, the pole should also be raised. (This is usually not associated with trimming the pole forward as the apparent wind, in a gust, initially moves aft, and later, unless the boat planes or surfs, when the boat speeds up, shifts but minimally forward).

Very Light Air

Maintain sail shape despite minimal aerodynamic lift.

Heel the boat to leeward to sag the mainsail and spinnaker into a lifting shape.

Drop the jib. Eliminate any interference with the flow of air onto and off the spinnaker.

Hold the main boom up (by hand or with some sort of topping lift) to keep the main leech open.

Change to a small, light spinnaker.

Use the spinnaker which is most likely to retain shape in the presence of minimal lift, that is, one that has the smallest area, is made of the lightest cloth, and is the driest. A spinnaker only functions when it is expanded; folds of nylon surrounding the jibstay do more harm than good. If it will not fill, drop it.

Hoist the spinnaker halyard fully.

Keep the spinnaker full at all times.

Watch the sail "like a hawk." Keep the luff folding so that the sail cannot stall.

Change to light spinnaker sheets that will not sag the leech and will permit the sail to lift in the slightest zephyr.

Hold the sheet up (and out of the water) by hand to encourage the sail to lift.

Raise and lower the spinnaker pole frequently to keep the luff full, the sail shifted to windward, and the leech open.

Keep the pole further forward than usual to keep the spinnaker and, particularly, its luff full (to facilitate attached flow).

Shift the crew weight carefully to avoid disturbing the sail.

Do not jibe except when the spinnaker is full (in a gust). Learn to jibe in light air so that the spinnaker will not collapse.

Periodically refilling the spinnaker is a waste of energy.

Keep the boat balanced.

If, by displacing the crew weight to leeward and forward, a significant weather helm develops, shift that weight farther aft.

Usually, however, with the minimal forces involved, it should be possible to keep the crew weight far forward (at least one crew member forward of the mast) and to leeward without creating a windward yawing moment.

If the spinnaker will not remain full, drop it and rehoist the jib.

Ease the backstay, provide "pre-bend," remove mainsheet pressure, or do whatever else is necessary to allow the jibstay to sag.

Attach the spinnaker halyard to the deck at the jib tack and pull the mast forward to increase jibstay sag.

Hold the jibsheet in the hand to encourage the jib to lift, to keep the leech open, and to modify the angle of incidence continuously. Care in the trim of the jibsheet is the most important determinant of success in very light air both because the jib is the first source of lift in the most minimal airflow and because the jib becomes the best of all telltales by indicating the direction of that flow.

Steer the boat as little as possible. Change the sail trim, spinnaker sheet, or jibsheet to adapt to changes in wind direction and velocity. Only after the trim is correct and the boat is responding with increased speed should the course be modified to adapt to new conditions.

Do sail up in the lulls, down in the gusts; go high initially if the wind is increasing, low if it is dying, but don't chase wind patches. Assume an approximate course, stick to it, and concentrate on sail trim.

HEAVY AIR REACHING

PROBLEMS

Maintain maximum speed despite heeling, weather yawing moment (and the risk of broaching), the presence of waves, and continuous variation in the angle of incidence.

SOLUTIONS (Fig. 7.4)

Decrease heeling and weather yawing moment by keeping the mainsail flat, twisted, and at the lowest possible angle of incidence and by keeping the spinnaker flat and trimmed close to the boat at the lowest possible angle of incidence.

Surf on wave faces whenever possible.

Trim the spinnaker sheet and vang (or mainsheet) continuously to keep both sails at the lowest possible angle of incidence despite rolling, pitching, and speed variations.

7.4. Heavy air reaching trim. Note in heavy air that the spinnaker is flatter —the pole farther aft, the sheet tighter, the halyard fully hoisted—its luff folding, and its leech open and flat.

RESPONSES

Decrease Heeling

Retain windward mainsail trim: flat, twisted, and draft forward. Keep the mast bent and the outhaul and Cunningham tensioned.

Ease the traveler all the way to leeward. Tension the vang sufficiently to control the leech; use the mainsheet to control the angle of incidence.

Ease the vang sufficiently so that the leech is well twisted and flexible (adaptable to rapid variations in the angle of incidence).

Trim the spinnaker close to the boat, with the halyard fully hoisted and the pole trimmed as far aft as possible: reduce the heeling moment as well as the windward yawing moment.

Set the pole sufficiently low that the leading edge of the spinnaker is under sufficient tension to pull the draft forward and permit the leech to be flat, open, and slightly twisted.

Maintain Balance—Decrease the Weather Yawing Moment *(Fig. 7.5)*

Keep the mainsail flattened through continued mast bend and outhaul tension.

Keep the jib full but trimmed outboard.

Keep the draft forward in the main, aft in the jib.

7.5. Yawing balance while reaching. Note location and direction of aerodynamic and hydrodynamic forces and the likelihood of their malalignment.

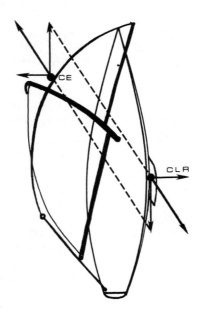

Keep the crew hiking and sufficiently far aft so that the bow is kept out of the water.

Keep the spinnaker guy, pole, and luff trimmed as far aft as possible. Keep the sheet eased so that the luff is continually collapsing. Keep the pole sufficiently down so that the draft in the spinnaker is shifted forward and the leech is open.

Stabilize the Boat Prior to Maneuvers

Keep the boat upright and the bow out of the wave ahead particularly prior to hoisting, dousing, jibing, and turning.

SURFING—PREPARATION

Minimize hydrodynamic resistance:

Eliminate the weather yawing moment

Keep the boat bolt upright through appropriate hiking and sail trim

Steer with but minimal rudder action (until moment of surf); that is, use shifts of crew weight to alter hull immersion

Maximize driving force:

Use the sails at the lowest effective angle of incidence and the highest possible sheeting angle so as to direct aerodynamic force more forward

Head down: bear away so as to direct aerodynamic force more forward

Keep the sheeting angle, twist, and sail fullness in a compromise status which produces the greatest possible aerodynamic force without an undue increase in heeling or windward yawing moment

SURFING—TECHNIQUE

Head up on the back of a wave to gain speed (but not until the previous surf has dissipated because heading up at high speed with the bow buried will almost certainly result in a broach). Ease the vang (or mainsheet) if necessary, to prevent heeling. Keep the spinnaker luff on the edge of breaking. Hike *hard*.

As the bow emerges on the wave face, jerk the tiller to windward (to break the frictional resistance), bear away, and, if possible, throw the crew weight forward (ooch).

Pump the guy aft to increase (briefly) the angle of incidence and the aerodynamic force.

Trim the spinnaker sheet, as necessary, to prevent the luff from collapsing (as the boat picks up speed). Trim the vang (or mainsheet).

Head down into the deepest "hole" (deepest depression) in the neighboring wave formations.

The combination of the increased aerodynamic force (from the improved orientation of the spinnaker, the guy pump, and the decreased sheeting angles), the decreased hydrodynamic resistance (from the hiking to upright position, the tiller jerk, and the ooch), the improved slope drag (the gravity/buoyancy relationships on the wave face), and the forward movement of the water in the wave face should result in surfing.

Maintain the surf through optimal spinnaker sheet ease, vang tension, hiking, and bow-down attitude (always dive into the "holes") for as long as possible. When speed is sufficient, surf through the next wave crest (with just a slight deviation to windward), hike, pump, jerk the tiller, and ooch onto a new surf, or, if the surf dissipates, await another wave and repeat the above process from the beginning.

TRIM THE SPINNAKER SHEET AND THE VANG CONTINUOUSLY

Keep the spinnaker luff collapsing at all times. One crew member (if possible) should have no other responsibility (except for contributing to the guy "pump" periodically). The more the spinnaker is "aimed" ahead rather than to leeward, the faster the boat will go, the more readily it will surf, and the less likely it will broach.

Keep the vang trimmed continuously (if possible) so that the boat is always bolt upright; ease whenever it starts to heel, trim in whenever the crew starts to drag in the water; ease whenever the boat heads up the back of a wave, trim in whenever the boat bears away down a wave. When in doubt, ease it; the boat will surf with the main ragging but it will never surf heeled.

PLANING

If the boat will plane, bear off until it planes and *then* look around to see where the boat is going. If in order to plane the boat must be headed below the rhumb line and/or the spinnaker must be set, head below it and set the spinnaker. Once planing, the boat can be brought back to a higher course than would have been possible in the absence of planing (so that the boat may be able to lay the rhumb line after all). Even if the rhumb line cannot be laid, a two-leg reach, part planing, part high on the wind without the spinnaker, will be faster.

Sail trim for planing is the same as for surfing (above).

THE INTENTIONAL BROACH

Move the crew weight aft while hiking maximally.
Release the vang and the mainsheet.
Release the spinnaker sheet.
Head up.
When a sufficient move to weather has been achieved:

Bear away
Trim vang and mainsheet gradually
Trim spinnaker sheet only after boat is back on course, upright, and moving

Beware of releasing mainsheet and vang excessively (avoid bearing away into a broach to leeward!).

RECOVERING FROM A BROACH (REACHING)

Recognize whether the boat can be brought back on course easily, with difficulty, or (almost) not at all.

Easily

Release vang and mainsheet
Bear away: if no response, release spinnaker sheet

With Difficulty

Release vang and spinnaker sheet completely
Luff until boat comes upright

Bear away
Trim vang gradually
Trim spinnaker sheet only after boat is back on course, upright,
    and moving

Not at All (to Windward)

Despite releasing vang, mainsheet, and spinnaker sheet, boat
refuses to bear away, remains blown over, and cockpit fills:

Never release the guy
Trim spinnaker sheet
Release spinnaker halyard and continue to trim spinnaker sheet
Gather in spinnaker to leeward as boat rounds up further and
    comes upright
Bail, or bear away and bail automatically

8
Special Conditions: Running

LIGHT AND MODERATE AIR RUNNING

PROBLEMS

Maintain maximum speed made good downwind (toward the leeward mark) by achieving the greatest possible speed over the shortest possible course. A compromise must be made continuously between sailing faster but longer and sailing slower but shorter. This compromise is best achieved by always sailing the jibe which when sailing close to the rhumb line is most headed and/or the jibe which keeps the boat in the strongest streaks of wind.

SOLUTIONS

Vary the course so as to keep the spinnaker full (to the optimal degree), sailing higher whenever the spinnaker sags, lower whenever it remains full. Jibe whenever this course is so high that the opposite jibe would better approximate the rhumb line at the same sailing angle *(Fig. 8.1)*.

Heel the boat to windward, drop the pole, and ease the sheet so as to shift the spinnaker to windward. Always keep the luff of the spinnaker at an angle of incidence which generates lift (evidenced by the luff lifting above and to windward of the pole end). It is the lift generated by the luff which keeps the spinnaker pulled to windward, full, and exposed to the air flow. Head the boat as high as is necessary to generate this lift. Trim the spinnaker pole as far aft as possible without overly flattening the sail *(Fig. 8.2A)*.

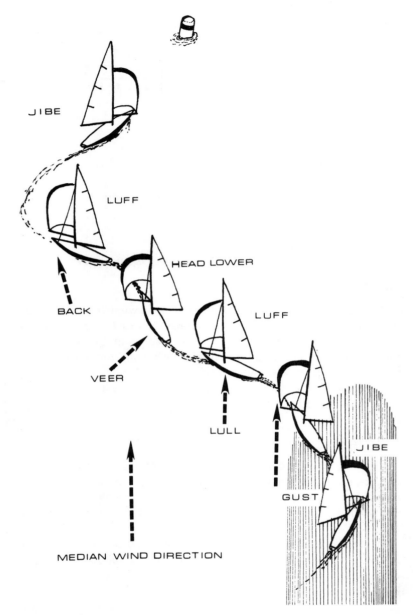

JIBE

LUFF

HEAD LOWER

BACK

LUFF

VEER

LULL

JIBE

GUST

MEDIAN WIND DIRECTION

8.1. Optimal running course. Note jibe to stay in gust, luff to respond to lull, alterations in heading to respond to shifts including a jibe when a lifting shift was beyond the median.

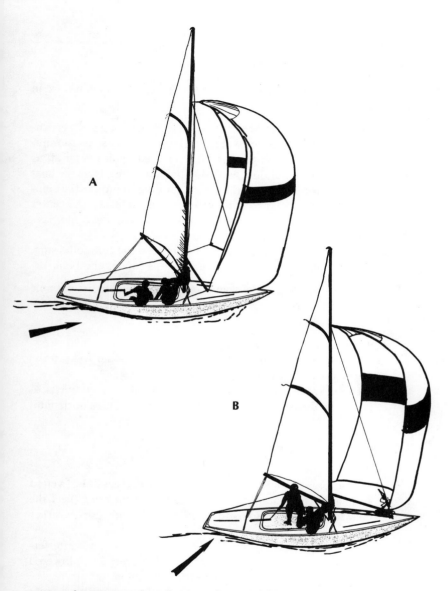

8.2A and 8.2B. Running trim—moderate and light air. Note mid-level of main and spinnaker pole perpendicular to wind, spinnaker shifted to windward by boat heeled to windward, spinnaker pole lowered and sheet eased, and sheet lead under boom in moderate air (A), in contrast to more reaching set of spinnaker in very light air (B).

RESPONSES—BASIC TRIM

Set both the spinnaker and the mainsail for maximum exposure in the stalled state.

Ease the mainsheet to project the mainsail within 15° if perpendicular to the apparent wind. Tension the vang so as to minimize twist. Trim the guy (and the spinnaker pole) as far aft as possible without unduly flattening the spinnaker. Heel the boat to windward and lower the spinnaker pole to induce the spinnaker to shift as far to windward as possible. Keep the center seam of the spinnaker vertical so that all the horizontal sections are symmetrical.

Ease the spinnaker sheet repeatedly to keep the luff collapsing. Lead the spinnaker sheet down amidships (under the boom).

Set the upper portion of the spinnaker so that the largest possible area is at an appropriate angle of incidence to generate lift from the air flow passing above it.

Rake the mast forward maximally.

Ease the spinnaker halyard (if there is enough wind to keep the upper portion of the spinnaker horizontal).

Lower the spinnaker pole so that the spinnaker is symmetrical (which will contribute to keeping its upper sections horizontal and symmetrical).

Keep the boat in yawing balance:

Rake the mast forward.

Shift the crew weight forward, so as to decrease the wetted surface to the minimum possible, and to windward (heel the boat to windward), so as to counteract the increased weather yawing moment so occasioned.

Drop the jib (unless it is obviously functioning and not interfering with the spinnaker). It may work effectively when lowered halfway with its head full beneath the spinnaker.

Keep the mainsail moderately full with its draft aft:

Straighten the mast.

Ease the outhaul (moderately—avoid decreasing projected area).

Ease the Cunningham (completely).

Keep the boat stable:

Distribute the crew so as to minimize pitching and rolling. Use a spinnaker with flat edges that do not induce rolling. Flatten the spinnaker sufficiently to negate rolling.

MODIFICATIONS

Very Light Air *(Fig. 8.2B)*

As the wind velocity diminishes, in order to keep the spinnaker full and maintain the best possible speed made good downwind, the boat will have to be headed higher. In gusts the boat can and should be headed off (with the sails stalled). In lulls it should be headed up to attain aerodynamic lift with the main leech telltales flowing. Because, in very light air, boat speed is high compared with wind speed, the apparent wind moves forward, generates lift, and requires that the spinnaker pole be carried close to the jibstay.

Change to a small, light spinnaker. Use the spinnaker that is the smallest, lightest, and driest available.

Keep the spinnaker full at all times (see "Light and Moderate Air Reaching," p. 149).

Steer the boat as little as possible, chiefly by shifting crew weight. To adapt to changes in wind direction and velocity, change the spinnaker sheet trim initially, then change the course.

Set the main and the spinnaker for a beam reach. Position the pole near the headstay. Elevate the pole to keep the spinnaker sections symmetrical, as the clew starts to lift. Trim the mainsheet and vang to assure that all leech telltales are flowing.

Trim the spinnaker sheet to the aft lead (at the transom) and over the boom (around the leech). Keep the spinnaker sheet eased and the luff constantly collapsing. If the boat develops a leeward yawing moment, de-rake the mast (shift it aft) and hoist the halyard fully.

Gusts

Gusts tend to strike the surface and to move downwind along the surface for some distance. If the boat can be sailed, more than its competitors, in such streaks, it will be possible to sail a shorter course, more directly downwind, and at a greater speed. As a gust appears, the boat should be headed off and sailed at the stall (in the "Basic

Trim" mode). If the initial jibe is taking the boat across and out of the gust, the boat should be jibed (unless the angle is particularly poor). In very light air it pays to go for the gusts, to get the boat up to speed, and to keep it there—even if the boat must be sailed, periodically, at a large angle to the rhumb line.

Varying Wind Velocity

In light air, a critical angle of incidence exists beyond which the luff of the spinnaker stalls and, without any lift force, the luff sags and the entire sail collapses into vertical folds. The boat must always be sailed sufficiently high that the luff generates lift, shifts to the windward side of the boat, and holds the remainder of the spinnaker, though most of it is stalled, up, out, full, and exposed. However, the boat should be sailed no higher than is necessary to just achieve this effect (maximum lift is achieved just short of the stall).

So long as the spinnaker is obviously full, the ability of the boat to sail lower without collapsing the spinnaker should be constantly tested (lower is shorter). The spinnaker trimmer should ease the sheet until he sees that the luff is collapsing (to demonstrate that he has that leading edge precisely splitting the wind flow) and the helmsman should attempt to bear away until he sees that the luff is stalling and sagging (to see how low he can sail).

With each increase in wind velocity the boat should be headed off. The spinnaker trimmer must recognize that this is about to happen and should both bring the pole aft and ease the sheet as it happens. If, in light air, the spinnaker stalls, it will be very difficult to fill again. It is best to only bear away when the spinnaker luff is collapsing, that is, to call for a sheet ease and to see the collapse before bearing away. An excellent technique is for the helmsman to hold the guy and, as he bears away, to trim the pole aft. Hike, to heel the boat to windward, to immerse the windward bow, and to cause the boat to bear away may be combined with a trim aft on the guy. Together with the heel, this shifts the spinnaker to windward and prevents it from stalling.

In a lull the boat must be brought up higher on the wind, to keep the luff generating sufficient lift to keep the rest of the sail full. The spinnaker will, otherwise, collapse and be difficult to refill both because the lighter air will be less able to remain attached and because, after the boat speed diminishes, the apparent wind will shift aft. Initially, however, the apparent wind will shift forward, causing the spinnaker trimmer to sheet in, to prevent the luff from collapsing excessively in what appears to be a header. This is dangerous, as the uninitiated trimmer may overreact, sheet in excessively, and stall the luff when he should be easing the sheet to accommodate the lull. As soon as the trimmer unfolds the luff, the helmsman, recognizing the lull, should head up and the sheet trimmer should ease the sheet, both actions intended to prevent the stall which will, otherwise, ensue.

Once the boat is up, higher on the wind, with its speed preserved, or but minimally diminished, the pole may have to be eased forward and/or elevated and the sheet trimmed in to adapt to the new apparent wind angle.

SUMMARY—INITIAL RESPONSES

Gust: ease the sheet and bear away
Lull: trim the sheet slightly, then ease it and head up

Variable Wind Direction

Every boat has an optimal downwind sailing angle in a particular strength of apparent wind (just as it has an optimal upwind sailing angle). In general, faster boats will sail at lower sailing angles (for a given wind strength) than slower boats and all boats will sail at their lowest sailing angles when sailing in the conditions which result in their greatest speed. A continuum exists for a particular boat which requires that it sail at very high angles (broad jibing angles, 90° or more) in order to generate lift along the luff in very light air (or in a relatively strong, opposing current wind which makes the apparent wind lighter) and permits it to sail at progressively lower angles in increasing winds until its maximum (displacement) hull spread is reached. (Inasmuch as the course is but minimally lengthened by sailing up to 15° from the rhumb line, it is rarely appropriate to sail dead downwind.) At some wind strength above maximum (displacement) hull speed, if the boat is capable of planing, it must be headed up to a planing angle and then, as the wind increases further, borne away again to a progressively lower course.

In order to keep the boat at the optimum downwind sailing angle (appropriate to the wind strength), the boat must be headed up in lifts and off in headers without changing the spinnaker pole position. The major advantage of this technique is that it permits, with the aid of a compass, recognition of the time to jibe in wind shifts. If, with the pole fixed, the boat must be headed so high (in order to keep the spinnaker at the proper angle of incidence) that the opposite jibe better approximates the median dead downwind course or the rhumb line, it should be jibed. This technique is essential to sailing in oscillating winds, permitting appropriate jibing in the lifts (lifts beyond the median), analagous to tacking in headers to windward, so as to sail the shortest possible course to the leeward mark.

Jibing technique must be perfected so that the boat can be jibed whenever a jibe is indicated (to respond to the appearance of a shift or a streak of increased velocity) without any loss in speed, and without collapsing the spinnaker (see "Running Jibe: Adjustments, Light Air," p. 191).

HEAVY AIR RUNNING

PROBLEMS

Maintain speed and utilize waves despite the risk of broaching (to windward or to leeward) due to sudden increases in yawing moment occasioned by gusts, heeling and/or rocking, asymmetric immersion of the bow and/or pitching, abrupt changes in course, displacement of the center of effort of the sails, or oscillation of the spinnaker.

SOLUTIONS (Fig. 8.3)

Keep the boat stabilized and the sails flat.

Avoid abrupt alterations in yawing moment when altering course (to respond to waves, when jibing, etc.). Keep the sails trimmed at all times so as to provide a modest windward yawing moment and so as to avoid inducing vertical or horizontal oscillations.

RESPONSES (THEORETICAL)

Keep the boat upright, particularly when the bow enters the back of a wave or when the course is altered deliberately.

Alter course (for jibing, for instance) only when the boat is surfing and the bow is not immersed in a wave.

Prevent rocking. Do not allow the upper portion of the mainsail to become so full or be so oriented that it generates lift perpendicular to

8.3. Heavy air running trim. Note mast raked aft, but straight, boom only moderately displaced from centerline, pole aft and sheet trimmed hard, sheets led down amidships.

the long axis of the hull. Do not allow the spinnaker to become so full that it generates lift perpendicular to the long axis of the hull and oscillates.

Keep the main and the spinnaker trimmed flat so as to maintain a modest windward yawing moment (and so as to prevent rocking).

RESPONSES (PRACTICAL)

Keep the mast raked aft. Ease backstay, Cunningham, vang, etc., sufficiently to prevent compressive bending.

Keep the outhaul tensioned so as to decrease mainsail draft.

Hoist and douse the spinnaker only when the boat is stabilized with its bow up.

Trim the vang/mainsheet so that the mainsail is flat with little twist, the leech is flat, and the boom is approximately 45° off the centerline. A special knot should prevent the boom from going out too far (permitting it to be released "by the run" as the weather mark is rounded). A major cause of broaching while running is allowing the mainsail to be too far outboard, thereby generating athwartship lift.

Keep the crew weight equally distributed athwartships and ready to move fore and aft in order to keep the bow approximately level— bow down when riding up the back of a wave, bow up when surfing down the front.

Set the pole sufficiently far aft that the spinnaker is flattened across the jibstay and cannot oscillate. If oscillations persist, set the pole lower than usual.

Lead the spinnaker sheet and guy to the deck (or gunwhale) amidships (through the use of twings, hooks, or snatch blocks) to diminish oscillations.

Trim the spinnaker sheet so that the luff barely lifts and trim hard whenever it does.

SURFING

Decrease Resistance

Keep the boat approximately upright and approximately level.

Use slight variations in hull trim rather than rudder action to steer.

Keep Boat on Wave Face

Head up to accelerate through a wave back.

Bear away as soon as the boat's chest emerges onto a wave face and ride directly down the wave face. If the waves are short (and therefore slower than the boat), avoid running into the back of the wave ahead (sooner than necessary) by riding across the wave face. If the waves are long (and therefore fast), maintain whatever course that, through the combination of aerodynamic force and slope drag, provides the greatest speed and the longest tenure on the wave face.

Facilitate Surfing by Abruptly Diminishing Resistance

Hike hard to jolt the boat upright as the boat starts down a wave. Jerk the rudder to weather to break the hull free of attached flow.

Pump Sails

Pump (no more than three pumps per wave are allowed) the spinnaker. (The spinnaker is by far the more powerful sail and therefore the one which, if present, should be pumped.) Pump guy and trim sheet simultaneously as boat is hiked hard and borne away down the wave.

Pump mainsail *if* the helmsman can do so readily without compromising his steering or if a crew member can coordinate the pump precisely with the steering and with the pumping of the spinnaker. In spinnaker-rigged boats, steering and spinnaker pumping are so much more important that less than optimal mainsail pumping often does more harm than good.

Avoid Broaching

In very heavy air beware of abrupt course changes, pumps associated with excessive easing of the sheets (before or after), abrupt shifts in crew weight (particularly to windward), courses angled across the wave face which may be associated with heeling and asymmetric immersion of the bow, and running into the back of the wave ahead while heeled—all of which may be associated with broaching.

JIBING

Tension the twings (or place the spinnaker sheet under the boom) so that the sheets are no more than boom high at the shrouds.

Square the spinnaker (preferably to previously tested marks on the sheets) so that the pole (tack) and clew are equally far aft. Cleat both sheet and guy.

Stabilize the hull; keep the rig upright.

As the bow breaks through a wave crest, send the foredeck man forward but have him wait for an order before jibing the pole.

Bear away and, when the boat begins to surf, simultaneously:

Have the foredeck man jibe the pole

Have the middleman (or the helmsman) throw the boom across

Counteract the turn (bear away, down the wave again, on the new jibe) and simultaneously have the middleman (if available) grab the new spinnaker sheet and trim *hard.*

Reattach the pole to the guy (if not already accomplished) and to the mast. If the foredeck man has difficulty, have him wait until the boat is stabilized (don't take chances with shifting his weight in the bow). So long as the sheets are in *hand,* even without the pole, the sail will not oscillate significantly.

Ease the guy forward as the pole is pushed out and against the tack.

Once the jibe sequence is started, don't hesitate. Keep bearing away until the boom comes across. Have the middleman brace his feet, get an optimal grip on the sheet or vang (or the boom itself), and, using all his strength, throw it across. (The sheet and traveler car must, of course, be free to run—preferably to a knot—so that the boom is not restricted until it reaches its optimal position on the opposite jibe.)

RECOVERING FROM A BROACH

Recognize whether the boat can be brought back on course easily, with difficulty, or (almost) not at all. Broaches to windward are usually controllable; broaches to leeward ("death rolls") rarely.

Easily (to Windward)

Attempt to bear away; if no response:

Ease spinnaker sheet abruptly and bear away.

Beware of bearing away excessively and broaching to leeward; trim spinnaker sheet and flatten spinnaker before boat has borne away completely.

With Difficulty (to Windward)

Release spinnaker sheet; if no response and boat rounds up beyond true wind abeam:

Release vang and/or mainsheet.

Continue to head up, with spinnaker ragging, until boat comes upright.

Bear away, trim vang, and then, after boat is back on course, upright, and moving, trim spinnaker sheet (but before boat has borne away completely).

Not at All (to Windward)

Despite releasing vang, mainsheet, and spinnaker sheet, boat refuses to bear away, remains blown over, and cockpit fills:

Never release the guy.
Trim spinnaker sheet.
Release spinnaker halyard and continue to trim spinnaker sheet.
Gather in spinnaker to leeward as boat rounds up further and comes upright.
Bail, or bear away and bail automatically.

Not at All (to Leeward)

Boat wipes away to leeward, mast comes over to windward as boom points skyward, spinnaker pole goes underwater, water pours into cockpit from windward side. Recovery will be abrupt and disastrous:

Do not release sheet (or guy, of course). Usually sheet is trimmed (though not sufficiently) as broach occurs. Sheet in harder, if possible.
Release halyard. If boat is still heeled to windward, spinnaker should fall into water to windward and be recovered easily as the boat abruptly comes upright.
Do not attempt to resume sailing with spinnaker if boat is filled with water; it will only broach again.
If boat comes upright before spinnaker halyard can be released, sheet in hard (if not already done) and release halyard. Drag spinnaker down through rigging.
Never release halyard until sheet (and guy) are trimmed in. Otherwise spinnaker may fill far to leeward and hold boat over.
Bail, or bear away and bail automatically.

ROLLING *(Fig. 8.4)*

Cause

Excessive rolling is usually caused by the harmonic combination of two or three primary forces. Aerodynamic forces (the production of

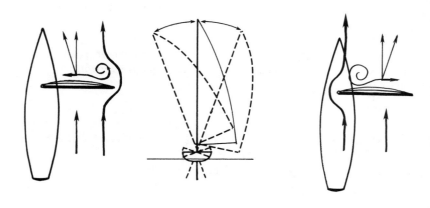

8.4. Rolling. The forces that facilitate and perpetuate rolling.

Karman vortices) may act to induce ("self-induced") rolling if a portion of a sail (particularly the spinnaker) is oriented so that a driving force operates athwartships. Rolling of a sail so oriented (an oscillating spinnaker or a mainsail eased out perpendicular to the long axis of the boat) will induce lift forces which accentuate lateral movement in both directions, rhythmically. Hydrodynamic forces may act to induce ("forced") rolling when waves cause the hull to roll rhythmically. When the periodic time of the "self-induced" roll approaches the periodic time of the "forced" roll, resonance occurs and the amplitude of the roll is greatly increased. If either or both of the "self-induced" and the "forced" roll rhythms match the periodic time of "free" oscillation (the oscillation which would occur if the boat were to be tipped laterally and then freed), resonance will be even more pronounced and the boat will probably roll into a capsize.

Control

Rolling can be diminished by interfering with resonance, by causing the periodic time of one type of oscillation (self-induced, forced, or free) to become different from that of the others. The free rolling period of a particular boat may be either longer or shorter than the self-induced and forced oscillations likely to be encountered. This difference must be discovered so as to determine how the free oscillation should be modified; that is, whether the rolling stability of the hull and/or the moment of inertia should be increased or decreased. Dampening of free oscillations is best achieved by a broad beam and a deep centerboard. A tender, but beamy hull will perform slower free oscillations (a stiff, narrow one faster oscillations). A large moment of inertia (the mass or weight times the distance from the axis of roll of the extremities of the boat; that is, the weight and distance offset of the mast tip and the centerboard or keel) will also increase the periodic time (slow the roll).

Solutions

Change the periodic time of aerodynamic "self-induced" rolling:

1. Hoist the spinnaker halyard fully and tension the sheet and guy, to flatten and reduce spinnaker oscillation.
2. Reduce the sheeting angle of the main boom. Jerk abruptly on the mainsheet.
3. Increase the vang tension to alter the fullness of the upper mainsail (which has the greatest arc of oscillation).
4. Alter the course so as to change the angle of incidence of the sails.

Change the periodic time of "forced" rolling:

Alter the course, usually by heading higher, so as to meet the waves at a different frequency (particularly appropriate if excessive rolling is intermittent, as this usually means that aerodynamic and hydrodynamic forces are involved and are recurrently resonant).

Change the periodic time of "free" rolling:

1. If the "self-induced" or "forced" oscillations are shorter than free oscillations, increase the moment of inertia by:
Lowering the centerboard (which also dampens the oscillations)
Standing up
Spreading the crew across the boat (one on each gunwhale)

2. If the "self-induced" or "forced" oscillations are longer than "free" oscillations, decrease the moment of inertia by:
Squatting in the cockpit
Raising the centerboard (which undesirably diminishes the dampening effect)
Concentrating the crew weight amidships

Oppose the roll by suitable balancing alternately swaying first one way then the other against the direction of the roll (opposing the angular velocity of the roll).

9

Maneuvers

TACKING

PROBLEMS

Preserve speed and emerge on the optimal course to windward, with no residual yawing moment, despite turning 70°–90° and luffing head to wind. Avoid excessive rudder angulation and increase in hydrodynamic drag.

SOLUTIONS *(Figs. 9.1A–9.1C)*

Use yawing moments created by altered hull immersion and sail trim to turn the boat. Shift the apparent wind appropriately by rolling the boat to windward prior to and after passing head to wind. Trim the sails to facilitate the turn and to generate maximum lift (aerodynamic force) from the altered apparent wind.

TECHNIQUE

Prepare the sails for maximal acceleration in recovery ("Go Gear," p. 105): ease the mainsheet (slightly) to increase twist and/or ease the backstay (slightly) to increase the fullness and shift the draft forward. Ease the jibsheet slightly (both to facilitate acceleration in recovery and to increase the weather yawing moment).

Allow the boat to heel by "unweighting" or by shifting the crew weight to leeward to cause it to heel. Shift the crew weight forward to shift the center of lateral resistance forward. The heeling and shift of the CLR create a windward yawing moment.

Pump the mainsheet or the main traveler abruptly to increase the weather yawing moment further; that is, create a sudden increase in aerodynamic force by the "pump effect."

9.1B. Tacking. Note jib fluttering but main full as boat heels to "windward" and boom is pumped in.

9.1A. Tacking. Note mainsheet and jibsheet eased and sails slightly twisted.

9.1C. Tacking. Note jib full and twisted and main full, twisted, and displaced from centerline on new tack.

Simultaneously, "power hike" or shift the crew weight to windward so as to roll the boat to windward. The combination of pumping and rolling shifts the apparent wind aft (almost to abeam) so that the boat, in response to the windward yawing moment, can turn almost head to wind without the sails luffing and, because of the "pump effect," without stalling. Speed is not only preserved but in light air may actually be increased, as the increased aerodynamic force provides an increased driving force.

Release the main traveler.

Keep the crew weight to windward until the boat is past head to wind (with the rig coming over on top of the crew). Then shift the crew weight rapidly across and over the rail on the new windward side.

Allow the boat to continue turning. Help it with a little rudder angulation to overcome the reversal of the yawing moment (as the boat heels and immerses the opposite side of its bow).

Hike to correct the heel and, as the boat reaches the appropriate course heading, bring the sails up into the wind. Create another "pump effect" with a shift of the apparent wind aft and an increase in the aerodynamic force so as to accelerate out of the tack.

Retrim the main traveler.

Retrim the jibsheet and the mainsheet and/or the backstay gradually. Do not bring leech back to original position until the boat is fully up to speed.

ADJUSTMENTS

Light Air

Ease the sheets and bear away slightly to develop maximum speed. Try to tack in a gust—not in a lull.

Allow the boat to heel by shifting crew weight to leeward and then, as the boat turns into the wind (due to the mainsail "pump"), shift the crew weight across the boat rapidly. Roll the rig and sails up and, as the boat reaches head to wind, over to a heel in the opposite direction.

Release the main traveler.

Allow the boat to remain heeled on the new tack to restore a windward yawing moment (in reverse) and to ensure that the sails settle in a stable shape which will produce aerodynamic lift.

Retrim the main traveler but keep the sheeting angle wide.
Assume a low heading (a wide heading angle).
Retrim the jibsheet and the mainsheet *very* gradually. Gradually head higher and trim sheets closer as, and if, speed increases.

Heavy Air

Reduce the hike—move inboard—momentarily and then throw the crew weight outboard to bring the rig through the maximum feasible arc.

Release the main traveler and/or the mainsheet.

Release the jibsheet *after* the boat passes head to wind (to ensure that the boat does turn past head to wind).

As soon as the boat passes head to wind, shift the crew weight inboard, across the boat, and out in a full hike on the opposite side—as rapidly as possible. Reach a full hike before the boat is fully borne away to the close-hauled course.

Retrim the main traveler gradually. Retrim the jibsheet gradually. But do not retrim either fully until the boat is up to speed.

(Alternative techniques are to ease and retrim the mainsheet or the vang—if vang sheeting is used—in light, centerboard boats.)

Recover in "go gear" with sails well twisted at wide sheeting angles and, if feasible, with their draft increased (backstay eased, vang eased) and shifted forward (backstay eased).

Tacking into a Leebow Position

As above, except be more careful to preserve speed by turning smoothly and gradually.

Complete the tack, with traveler down and sheets eased, by bearing away to a close-hauled course.

Retrim the main traveler amidships.

Pump the main and the jib by rapidly trimming both the jib and the mainsheets and roll the rig and the sails up into the wind to facilitate the pump.

Head the boat higher in synchrony with the pump to come up under the windward boat.

If the windward boat is not controlled in one's backwind after the initial luff, sail a scalloping course thereafter. Fall away to achieve maximum speed with the mainsheet trimmed to close the leech but with the main traveler and the jibsheet eased. Then, as the main traveler and the jibsheet are trimmed maximally, head up smoothly but rapidly. Continue to shoot approximately 10° above the close-hauled course, until the boat begins to slow; then bear away again with the main traveler and the jibsheet eased.

REACH-TO-REACH JIBE

PROBLEMS

Turn the boat without excessive rudder angulation or increase in hydrodynamic drag. Maintain spinnaker shape and stability throughout the turn despite the rapid shift in apparent wind. Reestablish attached flow on the spinnaker (in the reverse direction) as soon as possible. Prevent the development of excessive yawing moments (to leeward or to windward).

SOLUTIONS (Fig. 9.2 and Table 9.1)

Heel the boat to windward and ease the mainsheet to induce the boat to bear away (or maintain hike until it has begun to bear away).

Shift the spinnaker and the distribution of draft in the spinnaker to accommodate the shift in apparent wind direction.

Foredeck Man (or Men)

Keeps the spinnaker stabilized throughout the maneuver by easing the sheet and the windward twing gradually and by trimming the leeward twing prior to jibing. His positioning, with his hand on the pole preparatory to releasing it from the mast, is the key to the helmsman's order "now." Precise timing, of course, depends on the wave position, the mark location, other boats, etc. Once the pole is released the foredeck man must work as rapidly as possible to release it from the old guy, reattach it to the new guy, push it out and forward against the tack to flatten the new luff, and refasten it to the mast. He should be back in the cockpit, windward twing tensioned, hiking, sheet in hand, before the boat has completed its turn.

Middle Man (or Men)

Keeps the spinnaker stabilized and "choked-in," close to the headstay (after the foredeck man has released the twing). The guy must

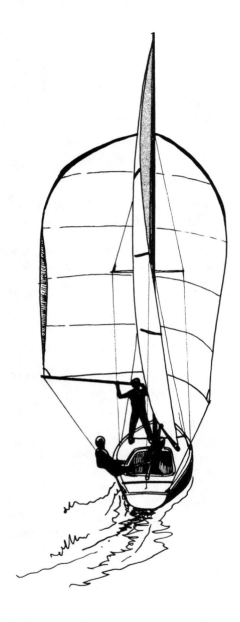

9.2. Reach-to-reach jibe—moderate air. Note spinnaker square across bow, foot indented by jibstay, spinnaker pole being pushed forward and out on new jibe, when boom is crossing the midline.

Table 9.1. Standard Technique, Reach-to-Reach Jibe

Foredeck	Middle	Helmsman	Spinnaker	Hull
Prepare	Hop into boat (after boat begins to bear away)	"Ready to jibe"	Shifts to windward (apparent wind aft and to leeward)	Bears away
—Ease sheet —Release windward twing (gradually) —Transfer sheet —Tension leeward twing (quickly)	Trim guy aft rapidly at first then gradually Cleat guy in running position (at mark)	Take sheet		
Up on deck (forward and to windward)		Stop bearing away (momentarily) Cleat sheet	Square (apparent wind dead aft)	Level
Release pole from mast*	Reach for boom*	"Now" bear away again*	Shifts to "old pole" side*	Bears away*

From sail
Attach pole
  To sail
  To mast
Return to cockpit
Trim new windward twing completely
Take sheet
Hike
	Throw boom across
	Go for sheet
	Sheet in *hard*
	Back across boat
	Trim sheet
	Hike (over guy)
	Transfer sheet
		(In heavy air counter-swing)
		Head up
		Ease guy
		Ease guy as twing is tensioned
		Cleat guy
		Hike
			(Apparent wind forward of abeam on "new" windward side)
			Shifts to "new pole" side
			(Apparent wind abaft of abeam)
				Heads up
				Ceases to turn
				On course

*Key to maneuver: These procedures must be done simultaneously. When the foredeck man removes the pole from the mast, the middle man reaches for the boom (preparatory to throwing it across) and the helmsman bears away (again). The procedures are essentially the same in a two-man boat except that the helmsman must also carry out the middle man's duties. (For twings read reaching hooks or similar devices to hold the guy down.)

be trimmed with great power and rapidity initially; then, as the trim angle becomes more efficient, the pole comes aft readily. Except in light air, it is best to cleat the guy (temporarily) so as to concentrate on bringing the boom across (slowly in moderate air, rapidly in heavy). As soon as the sail has filled on the new jibe, the new sheet (old guy) should be grabbed again and trimmed hard. This keeps the sail from oscillating and provides trim appropriate to the shift of the apparent wind forward of abeam on the new jibe (as the boat rounds up). The middle man should thereafter concentrate on trimming the sheet (keeping the luff on the edge of collapsing) until the foredeck man returns to relieve him.

Helmsman

The helmsman can (in addition to deciding when to initiate the jibing procedure and when to actually jibe) assist the foredeck man by taking the sheet as he goes forward, cleating the sheet temporarily (to keep the spinnaker stabilized as the boom comes across), and easing it (the new guy) gradually as the boat comes up on the wind. This should be done in coordination with the foredeck man. If he is having trouble, the helmsman can give him a quick ease on the guy, timed to match his effort to reattach the pole to the mast. Some guy should be held in reserve so that if the first effort fails a little more "guy ease" will still be available. (Ultimately, if all else fails, the sheet should be eased and the spinnaker luffed to permit easy reattachment of the pole.)

In two-man boats the helmsman must assume many of the middle man's duties. This usually means that he should cleat both sheet and guy prior to the boom being thrown across. He should immediately thereafter recover and trim the sheet. Subsequently, the guy can be eased through its cleat as the foredeck man reattaches the pole. Alternatively, the foredeck man can jibe the pole and reattach it to the mast before the boom is jibed, so as to be available to trim the sheet and the guy as the helmsman brings the boom across. This technique is less desirable in heavy air as it keeps the crew weight forward for an excessively long period and usually means that the spinnaker is freer to oscillate prior to and during the actual jibe.

ADJUSTMENTS

Light Air *(Fig. 9.3)*

Lower the jib, and assure that the spinnaker is full before the jibe is initiated.

Feed the old sheet out as the old guy is trimmed in. The lighter the air, the greater the shift in apparent wind created by the turn and therefore the more the sheet will have to be fed out and the more the guy will have to be trimmed in.

Bring the boom across gently (hold it amidships temporarily) to avoid disturbing the spinnaker and to permit what little airflow exists (when the boat is dead before it) to reach the spinnaker.

Ensure that the sheet is trimmed rapidly so as to bring the entire sail to the new leeward side of the headstay before the turn is completed. It is far worse to have some of the sail aback, to windward of the forestay, than stalled to leeward.

Push the pole out and forward against the new tack so as to open and flatten the new leading edge as soon as possible.

Luff the boat high into the wind (particularly if the new sheet has been overtrimmed during the turn) and trim the new guy back, if necessary, so as to reestablish attached flow on the leeward surface of the temporarily stalled spinnaker.

Ensure at the completion of the turn that the main (and the jib, if it has not been lowered) is luffing or, at least, is not stalled. This permits the spinnaker to refill without the disturbance of eddies from the other sail and avoids an excess weather yawing moment.

Heavy Air

Ideally, use heavy air running jibe technique (see "Heavy Air Running: Jibing," p. 173; "Running Jibe: Adjustments, Heavy Air," p. 191).

Alternatively, in close quarters, use the "Rag Jibe" technique; that is, conduct the jibe according to standard reach-to-reach technique except as follows:

1. Bear away and square the spinnaker as standard.
2. Release the pole from mast and sail.
3. Trim the old guy (new sheet) as hard and as rapidly as possible until the spinnaker is entirely to the new side of the headstay and cleat the sheet near the reaching position. Cleat the new

9.3. Reach-to-reach jibe—light air. Note spinnaker largely to leeward on new jibe, pole forward almost to jibstay, new sheet trimmed close, while boom is held on the centerline.

guy at the reaching position (permitting the new tack to go forward to the headstay) rather than at the running position. Reattach the pole to the new guy and the mast as the old guy (new sheet is being trimmed in). Throw the boom across.

4. As the boat rounds up to the new course, ease the sheet until the spinnaker is ragging. Complete the pole attachment (if necessary).

5. When the foredeck man returns to the cockpit, takes the sheet, adjusts the twings, etc., and everyone hikes, sheet in, fill the spinnaker, and go.

Cautions: Ensure that the new guy is cleated at the appropriate mark; disastrous broaches are assured by a loose guy. Overtrim the sheet (to match the guy position) during the jibe so as to keep the spinnaker close to the boat and free of oscillations.

RUNNING JIBE

PROBLEMS

Turn the boat without excess rudder angulation and increase in hydrodynamic drag. Maintain spinnaker shape and stability throughout the turn despite rapid and reversing shifts in the apparent wind. Increase the aerodynamic force as the boom is brought inboard.

SOLUTIONS *(Table 9.2)*

Heel the boat alternately to windward to induce it to bear away and then to windward on the new jibe to counteract the turn after the jibe is completed.

Shift the spinnaker and the distribution of the draft in the spinnaker to accommodate shifts in the apparent wind direction.

Pump the mainsail by rapid trimming (through reduced mainsheet or vang purchases or by pulling the boom itself inboard and across as the boat bears away). An aerodynamic force (with a vector operating forward) is created by this pump: the apparent wind (for the mainsail) is brought abeam and attached flow (from a stalled state) is initiated. (Such pumping is illegal except for the purpose of initiating surfing or planing or when integral to a jibe or tack, but is then highly effective.)

Table 9.2. Standard Technique, Running jibe

Foredeck	Middle	Helmsman	Spinnaker	Hull
Prepare / Set twings / Leap onto deck	Take sheet and guy / Keep weight amidships	"Ready to jibe" / "Go"	Squared	Level
Plant outer foot near windward gun'l	Trim guy	Assist in freeing sheet	Shifts toward "old pole" side	Bears away
		Shift weight to windward to aid bearing away	(Apparent wind to leeward)	
Detach pole from mast / Detach pole from sail	Continue to feed old sheet out and trim old guy in (as necessary to keep sail full)	Bring boom across (gently in light air, rapidly in moderate)	Jibes	Ceases to turn
Shift weight to opposite gun'l			Shifts toward "new pole" side	Bears away in reverse
Reattach pole to sail (push out and forward)	Trim new guy rapidly / Ease new sheet	Take guy	(Apparent wind reverses)	
Shift weight amidships / Reattach pole to mast / Return to cockpit / Take sheet / Trim, ease, or pump (as necessary)		Adjust course (as necessary) / Cleat guy	Stabilizes in normal position	Assumes proper course

ADJUSTMENTS

Light Air

Assure that the spinnaker is full before the jibe is initiated (jibe in a strong streak).

Feed the old sheet out and trim the old guy in. The lighter the air, the greater the shift in apparent wind created by the turn and therefore the more the old sheet will have to be fed out and the more the old guy will have to be trimmed in. In very light air the apparent wind may shift from nearly dead astern to abeam to "leeward" as the boat bears away and then gradually more aft as the turn slows and finally ceases.

Continue the "bearing away" in very light air until close to a beam reach (with the pole near the headstay). Counteract the "bearing away" in light to moderate air by a shift in crew weight to the new windward side when the jibe is completed.

Bring the boom across gently (hold it amidships temporarily) in very light air to avoid disturbing the spinnaker and to permit what little airflow exists (when the boat is dead downwind) to reach the spinnaker. In moderate air pull the boom across dramatically (so as to pump the main) in synchrony with the shift in crew weight that heels the boat to windward.

Push the pole out and forward against the new tack so as to open and flatten the new leading edge as soon as possible.

Free the new sheet (the old guy) to prevent stalling as soon as the boat ceases to turn (gradually in very light air, abruptly in light to moderate).

Trim the new guy rapidly in light to moderate air as the turn abruptly ceases, the crew weight shifts to the new windward side, and the boat bears away in the reverse direction.

Heavy Air

Tension the twings (or place the spinnaker sheet under the boom) so that the sheets are no more than boom high at the shrouds.

Square the spinnaker (preferably to previously tested marks on the sheets) so that the pole (tack) and clew are equally far aft. Cleat both sheet and guy.

Stabilize the hull; keep the rig upright.

As the bow breaks through a wave crest, send the foredeck man forward but have him wait for an order before jibing the pole.

Bear away and, when the boat begins to surf, simultaneously have the foredeck man and the middleman (or the helmsman) throw the boom across.

Counteract the turn (bear away, down the wave again, on the new jibe) and simultaneously have the middle man (if available) grab the new spinnaker sheet and trim *hard.*

Reattach the pole to the guy (if not already accomplished) and to the mast. If the foredeck man has difficulty, have him wait (don't take chances with shifting his weight in the bow). So long as the sheets are in *hard,* even without the pole, the sail will not oscillate significantly.

Ease the guy forward as the pole is pushed out and against the tack.

Once the jibe sequence is started, don't hesitate. Keep bearing away until the boom comes across. Have the middle man brace his feet, get an optimal grip on the sheet or vang (or the boom itself), and, using all his strength, throw it across. (The sheet and traveler car must, of course, be free to run—preferably to a knot—so that the boom is not restricted until it reaches its optimal position on the opposite jibe.)

SPINNAKER HOIST

PROBLEMS

Hoist and fill the spinnaker as rapidly as possible so as to create additional aerodynamic force and accelerate along the course.

PREPARATION

Prepare the spinnaker in a bin, roll, turtle, or launcher so that it will not twist during the hoist. Provide swivels on the halyard and on both sheets to facilitate untwisting.

Raise the pole. Trim the guy down with a hook or twing or trim the pole downhaul forward so as to prevent the pole from riding aft as the guy is trimmed. (Modify the pole end to reduce friction.)

As the mark is rounded, ease the jib (or lower it) so that it is not stalled. Eddies from a stalled jib will prevent the spinnaker from filling and lifting.

Ensure—by easing the main until it luffs, trimming the jib for optimal power, and bearing away sufficiently so that the boat is upright—that there is little residual yawing moment as the spinnaker is hoisted.

TECHNIQUE—GENERAL

On command, and as rapidly as possible, do the following.

Hoist the halyard and trim the guy simultaneously (prevent the sail from twisting).

Call the halyard "up" when it is cleated in position. Overtrim the guy until the tack is against the pole and the luff is luffing. Then ease the pole to the optimal position (to assure attached flow when the sheet is trimmed).

Position the crew appropriately.

Trim the spinnaker sheet sufficiently to fill the spinnaker. Avoid overtrimming.

Bear away so as to accelerate as the spinnaker fills.

ADJUSTMENTS

Light Air

Bear away gradually so as to preserve speed.

Ease the jib and drop (or roll) it as soon as possible.

Overtrim the guy (pull the sail into the wind) so as to obviate stalling, but recognize that the apparent wind (due to preserved boat speed) is farther forward than might be expected. Ease the sheet until the sail luffs, then sheet in.

Maintain a course high on the wind until the spinnaker fills and the boat is up to speed.

Do not bear away to jibe (unless tactically necessary) until the boat is up to speed.

Heavy Air

Bear away to a broad reach but not to dead downwind. Stabilize the hull before hoisting.

Free the sheet as the sail is hoisted. Avoid filling the sail before the halyard is cleated so as to avoid creating a major yawing moment if the sail fills while still away from the boat (with the halyard eased).

Sheet in *only* after the crew is properly positioned (on a reach—hiking).

TWISTING

Ease the halyard abruptly while pulling down on either the luff or the leech.

If the sail doesn't untwist, lower it completely (release the tension on the halyard and sheets completely) and untwist it by hand.

REACHING SET (Fig. 9.4)

Hoist (or position) the pole before rounding.

Bear away to a stable course so that the boat is upright and has little residual windward yawing moment. (Ease the main sheet completely and continue hiking during the rounding.)

Ease the jibsheet gradually, keeping the jib at the optimal trim to reduce the windward yawing moment. Finally, release to a stopper knot (or to some other automatic device to achieve an approximate reaching set) to ensure that the jib is not stalled as the spinnaker is hoisted.

Hoist the halyard and trim the guy aft simultaneously. Trim the guy until the tack is approximately 1 foot further aft than is considered to be appropriate. The guy will stretch after the sail is fully loaded and further adjustment by easing is much less difficult than by trimming.

Keep the sheet eased with the sail luffing until the halyard and guy are properly positioned and cleated. Avoid overtrimming (particularly in light air) before the sail is hoisted, as once stalled a spinnaker is very difficult to unstall. Then, with the crew in their hiking positions, sheet in, bear away, and go.

SPINNAKER DROP

PROBLEMS

Drop spinnaker on the desired side of the boat with as little decrease in speed as possible (in time to prepare for subsequent leg).

PREPARATION

Determine well in advance on which side (and whether to windward or to leeward) the spinnaker will be dropped.

Reset the jib (if lowered).

Set all controls, except the jib and mainsheets, for the wind direction, wind velocity, and wave and dirty air conditions to be expected on the subsequent leg. (In light air be gentle, particularly in reraking the mast.)

If the spinnaker is to be dropped to windward, remove the pole (or jibe it, without attaching it to the spinnaker) so that it will be out of the way. Hold the guy out and down (mimicking pole) until ready to drop.

9.4. Reaching spinnaker set. Note guy almost to pole end before spinnaker is fully hoisted, jib eased and luffing, and spinnaker sheet eased so that spinnaker is luffing.

TECHNIQUE

On command, and as rapidly as possible, do the following.

To Windward

Release halyard—so as to allow sail to blow away from rigging, drop quickly to near water level, and be gathered in without disturbing the airflow over jib and main.

Release sheet.

Pull foot around the headstay (keep the foot above the bow—avoid sailing over spinnaker!).

Pull sail down and into cockpit.

Remove pole.

To Leeward

Into Launching Shute
  Release halyard, sheet, and guy (in that order) as retriever line
    is pulled in.

In Light Air or on Broad Reach or Run
  Release halyard and guy (in that order) and pull in sheet (from
    behind shrouds on reach, ahead of shrouds on run).
  Pull sail down and into cockpit.

On Close Reach in Moderate Air *(Fig. 9.5)*
  Cleat sheet (so that sail can be controlled from leeward twing).
  Release guy. Allow sail to stream aft and to leeward from
    cleated halyard and twing (or sheet).
  Release halyard.
  Pull twing in and sail down and into cockpit.

On Close Reach in Heavy Air ("Halyard Drop")
  Trim sheet hard and cleat so as to stall spinnaker.
  Release halyard.
  Pull twing in and following along leech pull sail down and into
    cockpit.
  Release guy when leech is in hand and sail is under control.

Cleanup

Remove pole (if not already removed).

Check appropriateness of all elements of sail trim.

Trim and cleat sheets, twings, and halyard (particularly those which may be dragging in the water).

ADJUSTMENTS

Light Air

Drop to leeward, if at all possible, and release halyard well ahead of guy, to avoid disturbing airflow over jib and main.

Be gentle, with body movements as well as spinnaker manipulation, so as to permit jib and main to develop attached flow.

Keep crew weight to leeward, jib and main twisted, and jibstay sagged until boat is up to speed.

9.5. Leeward spinnaker drop. Note spinnaker guy released sufficiently so that spinnaker can "flag" dead to leeward and be retrieved by twing.

Heavy Air—Reaching

To exploit the potential advantages of using a spinnaker on a "two-leg reach" (with and without the spinnaker), it must be possible to lower the spinnaker without diminishing speed. Each member of the crew must know his specific duties in advance so as not to distract his fellows from theirs (particularly not distract those responsible for continued speed—helmsman and jib trimmer).

Prior to dropping the spinnaker set all controls, including the jib-sheet, for the course ahead (remaining segment of reach).

Coil (or clear) all lines (halyard, guy, sheet) that must be able to run before releasing any.

Bear away, if possible, as spinnaker is dropped. Use techniques such as halyard drop if boat cannot be borne away.

Heavy Air—Running

TO LEEWARD

Allow pole to go forward by releasing guy partway and trimming sheet so as to blanket spinnaker behind mainsail (avoid oscillations due to filling spinnaker far from boat as halyard is released). Hold guy, to keep spinnaker tack at headstay, as halyard is released. Gather in sail to leeward using sheet and twing. Release guy after sail is under control.

TO WINDWARD

Release sheet as spinnaker pole is removed from mast. Simultaneously, pull pole inboard and pull sail around to windward of headstay. When tack is in hand, release halyard and pull sail down into cockpit.

SPINNAKER CHANGE

If only one spinnaker halyard and one set of sheets are available, a quick change requires the following organization.

1. Preparation:
   Each crew member understands his responsibilities.
   The drop will occur in an organized fashion with restraining lines free to run.
2. Selection of an appropriate time so that minimal loss in speed will occur.

While jibing: boat loses in recovery anyway.

In lull: while bearing away or sailing dead downwind (due to tactical needs).

3. Organization of new spinnaker:

Should be confined in roll or turtle and fastened in place near leeward gun'l or on new leeward (old windward) gun'l, if change is to be made during jibe.

As old spinnaker is dropped, crew can easily find corners of new spinnaker and transfer lines.

As soon as all lines are attached, that state should be announced so that hoist and guy trim can follow immediately.

Clean up old spinnaker only after new one is properly set and boat is moving at optimal speed.

SPINNAKER SET WHILE JIBING

PROBLEMS

Hoist and fill the spinnaker as soon after rounding the weather mark as possible while bearing away, jibing, and rounding up on a new jibe.

SOLUTION (Fig. 9.6)

Set and fill the spinnaker to windward on the initial jibe, with the pole to leeward, so that it will remain full during the jibe and be properly oriented after the jibe.

VARIATIONS

1. Set on the old jibe.

Wait for the spinnaker to fill and, in light air, for the boat to be up to speed and then jibe.

2. Set on the new jibe with the pole hoisted.

Hoist (or position) the pole to leeward on the approach to the mark.

Organize the spinnaker for hoisting as the mark is rounded.

Begin to hoist and to trim the guy (to leeward) as soon as the boat has borne away beyond wind abeam and fill the

9.6. Spinnaker jibe set. Note spinnaker pole set to port with spinnaker filled to starboard as boom reaches centerline.

spinnaker (without its pole) to windward (preferable in light to moderate air).

OR Begin to hoist and trim the guy after the boat is fully borne away and fill the spinnaker after jibing, on the new jibe (preferable in heavy air to avoid broaching).

Keep the sheet eased until the spinnaker fills and begins to luff at its new windward edge, then trim in just enough to prevent collapse.

Drop (or roll) the jib as soon as possible, prior to the jibe if possible. This is essential in light air (to permit the spinnaker to fill as the boat bears away and markedly reduces its apparent wind).

Jibe.

Overtrim the guy to create an apparent wind at the spinnaker's leading edge and then gradually ease the pole forward to an approximately correct position for the sailing angle.

3. Set on the new jibe without the pole.

Begin to hoist and to trim the guy (to leeward) as soon as the boat has borne away beyond wind abeam and fill the spinnaker (without its pole) to windward.

Drop (or roll) the jib as soon as possible, prior to the jibe if possible.

Jibe, but hold the boom approximately amidships until the pole is properly positioned.

Proceed as above.

Avoid jibing before the spinnaker is filled.

It is nearly impossible to pull the unfilled spinnaker around to windward of the forestay without a pole (particularly if the jib is up and the main is blanketing) so that it must be filled prior to jibing.

ADJUSTMENTS

Light Air

Set and fill the spinnaker on the initial jibe, with the pole to windward, unless there is a clear advantage on the opposite side of the course or the wind direction requires sailing the entire leg on the opposite jibe.

If a jibe is required, bear away gradually and smoothly and set the spinnaker to windward prior to jibing (with the pole positioned to leeward). Trim the guy (to leeward) and free the sheet sufficiently to fill the spinnaker before the jibe. As the apparent wind will be well forward due to the preservation of speed in the gradual turn, the spinnaker will not fill until the boat is well below true wind abeam.

Drop (or roll) the jib before jibing.

Bring the mainsail gradually amidships and hold it there during the jibe and until the pole is positioned and the spinnaker stabilized on the new jibe.

Overtrim the new guy and then ease it as necessary as the boat rounds up.

Keep the sheet eased with the luff breaking continuously.

Round up high on the new jibe to gain speed and assure attached flow before bearing away to the optimal course.

Heavy Air

Set on one jibe or the other, not while jibing. Set the pole before the spinnaker. Do not hoist while heading dead downwind. Retain a slight windward yawing moment during the hoist to avoid a disastrous leeward broach.

BEARING AWAY

PROBLEMS

To bear away (around the weather mark or astern of a crossing starboard tacker) from a close-hauled course to a reach or run while preserving speed as well as possible (producing the least possible drag).

SOLUTION (Fig. 9.7)

Decrease the windward yawing moment, increase the leeward yawing moment, and avoid excessive rudder angulation.

RESPONSES

Decrease the weather yawing moment.

Ease the main traveler and/or the mainsheet to reduce the angle of incidence of the mainsail (despite bearing away).

Decrease the power generated by the mainsail. Reduce heeling (to leeward).

Increase the leeward yawing moment.

Hike hard enough (shift the crew weight to windward sufficiently that the boat heels to windward, if possible). Ease the jibsheet to prevent the jib from stalling but keep it trimmed sufficiently to increase its angle of incidence (increase the power generated by the jib).

Avoid excessive rudder angulation.

To initiate the turn, ease the mainsheet and hike abruptly.

Use, in addition, whatever rudder angulation is necessary to steer the boat at a constant, gradual rate of turn around the mark or obstruction.

9.7. Bearing away. Note main traveler and mainsheet eased, crew hiking maximally and boat flat.

Keep the crew weight over the rail until the boat has borne away to an upright posture. Less and less rudder angulation will be necessary as the boat comes fully upright and turns beyond wind abeam.

When bearing away behind a crossing boat (unless, for tactical purposes, it is important to deceive her) begin the course angulation approximately two boat lengths away, aim for an amidships collision, and gradually bear away (or head up) to correct the course for a close astern pass. Every foot passed astern of the crossing boat is a foot lost. Head up smoothly but rapidly back to the close-hauled course and, in smooth water, to above close-hauled, while retrimming the mainsail rapidly. Trim the jib gradually, after the main, and, particularly in light air, allow the boat to heel so as to facilitate a windward yawing moment (until the boat has been brought up as high as is intended).

LUFFING

PROBLEMS

To luff (around the leeward mark, after passing astern of a starboard tacker, or when, in a leebow position, attempting to gain control of a weather boat) to a close-hauled (or higher) course while preserving speed as well as possible (producing the least possible drag).

SOLUTION (Fig. 9.8)

Increase the windward yawing moment, decrease the leeward yawing moment, and avoid excessive rudder angulation.

RESPONSES

Increase the windward yawing moment.
    Trim the main traveler and/or mainsheet to increase the angle of incidence of the mainsail (create a "pump" effect) despite heading up. (Increase the power generated by the mainsail.)
    Allow the boat to heel (to leeward).
Decrease the leeward yawing moment.
    Shift the crew weight to leeward so that the boat heels to leeward.

Trim the jibsheet very gradually (in synchrony with the turn) so that the jib is continuously luffing slightly, at a low angle of incidence. (Decrease the power generated by the jib.) *Do not allow the jib to stall.* Trimming it too rapidly will diminish the rate of acquisition of speed once the boat reaches close-hauled.

Avoid excessive rudder angulation.

To initiate the turn, trim the mainsheet and shift the crew weight (to leeward) rapidly. Use whatever rudder angulation is necessary to steer the boat at a constant rate of turn around the mark or obstruction. Preferably steer for a wide approach and a close departure.

Keep the crew to leeward until the boat is up to close-hauled. Less and less rudder angulation will be necessary as the boat approaches close-hauled.

9.8. Luffing. Note main traveler to windward of centerline, mainsheet tensioned to hook leech, and boat heeled (to leeward).

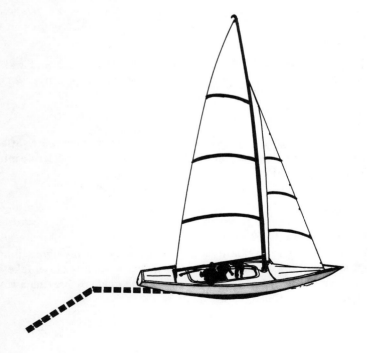

ADJUSTMENTS

When sailing a scalloping course to windward (in smooth water) or when attempting to gain control of a boat on the weather quarter, allow the boat to heel (slightly), trim the mainsheet (and traveler, if it is down) until the upper leech telltales stall, and head up, at a constant gradual rate of turn, until the jib luffs significantly. When the boat begins to slow, hike, ease the mainsheet, and bear away smoothly to the close-hauled course. Do not initiate another luff until the boat is fully up to speed.

The most important aspect of rounding the leeward mark is the departure, which should be at full speed, in clear air, and in the preferred direction. It is desirable to drop the spinnaker and prepare the boat as early as necessary to assure this outcome. The helmsman should be free and alert to take full advantage of any opportunity that develops—to shoot through a gap inside, to make a wide swoop outside, or to luff and tack immediately. The crew should maintain the appropriate angle of heel and the appropriate angle of incidence of the jib during any such modification of heading.

PASSING ON THE REACH

PROBLEMS

To pass to windward or to leeward despite backwind and wake from a boat ahead (or to prevent an opponent from passing).

SOLUTION

When advantageously positioned relative to an opponent, use variations in the apparent wind and wave and wake riding to accelerate into a controlling position.

RESPONSES

For an Attack to Windward *(Fig. 9.9)*

Position the boat so that it can move to the fastest possible sailing angle when an opportunity appears. When the reach is close, take a position to windward so that an attack can be made by bearing away to the fastest possible course.

9.9. Passing to windward. Note windward boat headed down, maximally hiked to keep it flat, and spinnaker guy and sheet ''pumped'' in.

When the reach is broad, take a position to leeward so that an attack can be made by heading up to the fastest possible course.

Attack when the wave conditions benefit the boat astern and hinder the boat ahead.

Use a wind wave to provide acceleration. Position the boat so that, with the acceleration due to the improved sailing angle and the wind wave, the boat will surge onto the face of the stern wave (wake) of the boat ahead.

Attack just as a gust or a wind wave appears (be alert to its arrival; keep watch to windward), before the opponent begins to accelerate and preferably when she is slowed in a trough.

For an Attack to Leeward *(Fig. 9.10)*

Position the boat so that it can move through the blanket zone of the boat ahead when an opportunity appears.

Never attempt to pass to leeward when on a close reach, only when the boat can be brought to a position abeam to leeward without entering the windward boat's blanket zone. Never attempt to pass within two boat lengths to leeward of a windward boat (so that, where crossed, the cone of blanketing will be narrow).

Hover (slow up, if necessary) just astern of the windward boat's blanket zone awaiting a forward shift of the true wind.

Attack when the true wind shifts forward and comes from ahead of the leeward boat or when the windward boat slows in a trough.

Head up to bring the apparent wind forward and ahead of the windward boat.

Expect to break through in light air (particularly in variable, puffy air) or in waves. Do not expect to break through in moderate air and smooth water.

Do not try to break through unless certain the attempt will be successful. To turn upwind under a windward boat and not get through is to be trapped, blanketed, and dropped astern.

To Prevent a Boat from Passing to Windward

Maintain a position to counter an attack: ahead and slightly to windward on a close reach, ahead and slightly to leeward on a broad reach.

To attain the same advantage, come up after the boat astern comes up, in coordination with the actual arrival of the gust or the wind

9.10. Passing to leeward. Note apparent wind of leeward boat crossing ahead of windward boat as the former luffs to a beam reach.

wave (not before). Come up no higher and maintain the high course no longer than the attacking boat.

Do not be misled into coming up sooner, higher, longer, or more frequently than the boat astern.

To Prevent a Boat from Passing to Leeward

Maintain a course as low as is possible to increase the deviation necessary for the attacking boat.

The boat ahead cannot bear away below her proper course (the course which will get her to the next mark most rapidly, usually taken to be the course sailed prior to the appearance of the attacking boat) when the boat astern (or to leeward) is within three lengths. Never allow the attacking boat to reach a position more than three lengths to leeward.

When an attacking boat is abeam to leeward (within three boat lengths), be alert (when the wind shifts forward and/or when she heads up) to head up with her.

TRIM

Use crew weight movement to steer (heel to leeward to luff and heel to windward to bear away) and to keep the boat at the optimal angle of heel.

In moderate to heavy air, shift the crew weight to windward prior to bearing away or to heading up. Have the crew over the rail (when appropriate) as the boat heads up, so that it can accelerate in the increased apparent wind.

In light air shift the crew weight to leeward prior to heading up (to create a windward yawing moment) and to windward prior to bearing away (to create a leeward yawing moment).

Use the mainsail to facilitate steering.

In light to moderate air trim the mainsheet (or traveler) prior to heading up (to increase the windward yawing moment) and ease the mainsheet prior to bearing away (to reduce the windward yawing moment).

Use the mainsail to facilitate acceleration.

Trim the mainsail abruptly to create a "pump effect" (do not repeat more than twice) as the boat starts down a wind or wake wave.

Retrim the spinnaker sheet and guy.

Ease the spinnaker sheet to assure that the luff is breaking prior to bearing away.

Trim the pole aft as the boat bears away. Ease the sheet further to keep the luff breaking and to prevent the luff from stalling.

Tension the spinnaker sheet abruptly just before and as the boat heads up to create a "pump effect."

Ease the pole forward as the boat heads up but no further than necessary.

Continue to trim the sheet as necessary to keep the luff just breaking.

Reset the pole for the altered course and decreased speed.

Continuously trim and ease the spinnaker sheet to adapt to the abrupt alterations in apparent wind as the wind velocity changes, the boat speed changes (due to changes in the wind and to wave riding), and the heading changes.

BLANKETING

PROBLEMS

To block the airflow to a boat ahead or to escape from the blanketing effect of another boat on a downwind leg.

SOLUTION

Vary the downwind course as necessary so as to interpose one's sails between the wind and an opponent's sails and so as to avoid the interposition of an opponent's sails between one's own sails and the wind.

RESPONSES

The priorities when sailing downwind should be as follows:

Sail the jibe taking the boat to the advantageous side of the course.

Sail the headed jibe, the jibe which takes the boat (at the optimal sailing angle) closest to the rhumb line.

Sail the jibe which keeps the boat in the strongest streaks of wind.

Sail the jibe which keeps the boat in clear air.

As all boats are trying to sail the same course (as indicated above), blanketing is likely to occur. Keep alert to the wind direction and to the position of one's opponents. Check both one's own masthead fly and those of neighboring boats. While the boat is sailed on the advantageous side of the course, on the headed jibe, and in the strongest streaks, its course must be continually modified to avoid (or induce) blanketing.

To Escape Blanketing *(Fig. 9.11)*

Bear away (preferable in moderate to heavy air).
  Shift the crew weight to windward.
  Before the boat is borne away, trim the spinnaker pole aft and ease the sheet. Keep the luff of the spinnaker collapsing. In light air do not allow the luff to stall. (Do not bear away so far that the luff sags.)
  Ease the mainsheet (to reduce the windward yawing moment —carefully in heavy air to avoid creating a major leeward yawing moment and a disastrous broach).
Head up (preferable in light air).
  Shift the crew weight to leeward.
  After the boat begins to head up, trim the sheet and ease the spinnaker pole forward. Trim the sheet just enough to prevent collapse, but keep the luff folding.
  Trim the mainsheet. Keep the mainsail from luffing if the boat does not heel but allow it to luff if necessary to prevent heeling.

To Induce Blanketing

Bear away or head up, as above, but more gradually. The more gradual the turn the less extra distance is sailed and the less speed is lost. The boat astern (as the aggressor) should be able to bear away or head up gradually while the boat ahead, uncertain as to the aggressor's intentions and unable to maintain as constant a watch, will be required to respond rapidly. The boat astern has the dual advantage of gaining when she induces blanketing and when she induces a rapid move to escape. The boat ahead, recognizing that each hazard is significant, must be alert both to blanketing and to the need for avoiding a rapid escape move.

9.11. Avoidance of blanketing. Note boat ahead facilitating its bearing away by heeling to windward and shifting the spinnaker to windward.

In light air an attempt to escape by bearing away from the optimal sailing angle will usually be disastrous as the sails will stall and the boat astern will sail on by with or without blanketing. However, in moderate to heavy air, bearing away is the better escape technique both because it shortens the downwind course and (with the boat at displacement hull speed) reduces speed but minimally and because the aggressor (by Rule 39) is limited from bearing away "when she is clearly within three of her overall lengths of a leeward yacht" (a yacht overlapped to leeward). Thus, there is a legal haven for the boat escaping to leeward; ultimately when the aggressor has caught up (bow abeam of transom) she is prohibited from bearing away further and must relinquish the blanket. There is no haven to windward; the aggressor astern can luff as high and as long as she wishes and may require the boat ahead (in order to escape blanketing) to sail far from her optimal course.

10
Organization

THE TRIM CHART

PROBLEMS

Reproduce, from prior experience in similar conditions, optimal sail trim. Develop an understanding of the modifications of sail trim appropriate to various and/or changing conditions (despite a possible lack of experience in those particular conditions).

SOLUTION *(Charts 3A–3C, see pp. 246–251)*

Maintain trim charts upon which can be recorded information gained by testing relative to other boats. Trim charts should be used to record, relative to wind velocity, the settings of the sail trim controls which appear to result in good performances. When experience in other wind velocities is subsequently acquired, it will be possible to interpolate optimal settings for intermediate and adjacent, but not experienced, wind velocities. Eventually, the chart (subject, of course, to correction) should indicate optimal settings for all controls in all wind velocities.

To the extent that the principles of sail trim (as outlined in this book) are understood, interpolation will be simpler and more likely to be correct. Such understanding, of course, enhances the accuracy of testing and makes more likely the recording of correct and significant information. Testing, particularly during competition, is fraught with misinterpretation.

LIMITATIONS OF A TRIM CHART

A trim chart should permit the maintenance of close to optimal sail trim and its restoration immediately after a change in conditions—

after the start, the leeward mark rounding, etc. It is a reduction in the frequency and duration of periods of far from optimal sail trim that makes the greatest difference in performance. However, the maintenance of a state of near optimal trim is more theoretical than practical, consequent to the many defects in the system of gathering data and to the many variables which prevent optimal trim from being recognized.

DEFECTS IN ASCERTAINMENT

Defects in Measuring the Wind Velocity

Even with sophisticated instrumentation, it is difficult to recognize the most significant factor, the percentage of time during which the wind blows at a particular velocity. In boats whose heeling is modified by hiking, the best measure of wind velocity is crew position. To the extent that the sails are trimmed "properly" and reproducibly, heeling force and the resultant shift in crew weight (from leeward gunwhale to windward full hike or trapeze) correlate with wind velocity. Crew position, to maintain the optimal angle of heel, is certainly the best indicator of aerodynamic force achieved, which is, after all, the variable that matters.

Defects in Recognizing Disturbed (Dirty) Air Effects

All airflow is irregular; the difficulty is in distinguishing how irregular it is. How significant is the backwind of the boat ahead, the pitching due to the waves at hand, the thermal turbulence ashore? Will similar conditions be recognizable in the future?

Defects in Distinguishing the Determinants of Performance

Performance depends upon many factors unrelated to, or only tangentially related to, sail trim: steering; yawing moments; righting moments; weight of the hull, rig, and crew; hull and sail surfaces; windage; functional capability of the running rigging; and inherent sail shape; at least.

Inherent sail shape is probably the most important variable among equally well managed one-design boats. No two sails are alike. Sailors deliberately purchase sails of different design. Sailcloth, despite the efforts of sailmakers to test new batches, varies markedly; hand con-

struction does not permit reproductibility. All sails deteriorate—
stretch, become fuller, shift the position of their maximum draft—and
some do so considerably more rapidly than others.

DEFECTS IN RECOGNIZING TRIM THAT IS OPTIMAL

Comparative Performance

If the performance of the boat being tested against is significantly
different from one's own or if the performance of the other boat
changes during the test, it will be difficult to determine which and
whose change is causing the observed effects. Testing during a race
is particularly unreliable, as the other boat is not only changing
independently but her helmsman is attempting to counter the im-
provements you are making.

If the other boat's airflow is different (and it always is)—stronger
or lighter, dirtier or cleaner, veered or backed—the change induced
in its performance will obscure and/or possibly reverse the effects of
changes in your sail trim.

Relationships between Trim Variables

Each trim variable depends upon many others. Optimal trim for the
jibsheet depends upon the jib lead position (fore and aft and lateral),
the jib luff tension, the position of the jib on the stay, and the jibstay
sag (which depends upon the backstay, mainsheet, and vang tension,
the shroud/spreader relationships, chocking, pulling, lower shroud
tension, etc.). Obviously, if one of these other trim variables is incor-
rect, the setting of the jibsheet which appears to give the best performance may not in fact be optimal. With rare exceptions, indeed, the
optimal settings which are recognized are only the best compromises,
the best corrections of all the other inappropriate adjustments. Constant reassessment is essential.

ATTRIBUTES OF A VALID OBSERVATION

1. A consistent change in performance observed repeatedly over
   prolonged periods in association with a particular change in
   trim.

2. A change in performance which is consistent with theoretical expectations. (Less jibstay sag *should* improve performance in moderate air and smooth water. If an observation is to the contrary, doubt it.)
3. A change in performance which is consistent with previous experience. A major advantage of a trim chart is that it facilitates interpolation. (If the optimal fore-and-aft mast bend for 12–14 knots is 6 inches and for 18–20 knots is 9 inches, then an observation that 7 inches is optimal at 15–16 knots is probably valid.)

THE NEED FOR MULTIPLE TRIM CHARTS

Each sail needs a different trim chart (no two sails are the same) and each chart should be modified as the sail deteriorates. (Beware "measuring in" a new, untested sail for a major regatta.) Most sails produce their best performance at some frequency of use between two to three occasions and ten to twenty occasions. Too few occasions obviates adequate testing; too many results in deterioration. (By the time you know how to use it, it's too late to do so!)

Each sail needs at least two trim charts, one for smooth water and one for waves. One could justify the production of additional charts for clean and for dirty air as well (i.e., four charts: clean air/smooth water, dirty air/smooth water, clean air/waves, and dirty air/waves). Fortunately, in smooth water, the boat's steadiness diminishes the effects of dirty air and in waves the air *is* dirty due to the waves. So two charts are usually enough. At first one chart, with a modifying factor for each column to permit adapting to the opposite condition, can be prepared. Later, the smooth water and the waves data can be separated onto two charts. Try to obtain data well outside the range of conditions for which the sail was designed. (Just because the sail was designed for light to moderate air in smooth water, doesn't mean you won't be caught out with it in 18 knots and big seas.)

Trim charts are not ordinarily prepared for reaching or running trim both because such trim is so difficult to quantitate *and* because variation in apparent wind strength and direction (due to variations in boat speed and heading) is so great. Offwind trim cannot be optimal, except momentarily, so it is reasonable to accept approximations which will, at least, intermittently be correct.

CONTROL SYSTEMS

RAKE

Significance
Determines sheet lead positions, sheet lengths for a given tension, backstay length, etc.

Method
To determine the rake when resetting the rig (changing masts, stays, etc.) and when comparing rake among several boats, establish a mark on the lower portion of the jibstay equal to the height of the jibstay-to-mast attachment above the deck. This position can be determined readily by swinging the jibstay back to the base of the mast. Because the curve of the wire, as it is held against the deck, interferes with accurate measurement, it is best to mark the mast and the wire 12 inches, or any fixed distance, above the deck. Thereafter, with the jibstay in place, rake and changes in rake can be measured as the distance from the mark on the jibstay to the deck (chain plate, gunwhale, etc.).

Visibility
Colored tape or nail polish can be used to designate one or more positions along the jibstay near the deck. (If the jibstay is not fully adjustable, similar marks may be used to designate pin positions in the chain plate.)

Very Light Air
Use maximum rake.

If rake is to be modified at all, it should be at its maximum in very light air so as to:

Attain maximum lift (swept back sailplan)

Reduce "tip losses" (eddies under the boom and jib foot) through the "end-plate effect"

Decrease leeward yawing moment and/or increase weather yawing moment at a time when (because of the minimal forces) a weather yawing moment is well tolerated.

Light Air

Use maximum rake.

Moderate Air

Use reduced rake (if necessary).

Permit maximum mainsheet tension (to close the leech) without two-blocking the sheet.

Heavy Air

Reduce rake (if necessary).

Permit increased mast bend (to flatten the mainsail and tension the jibstay) without two-blocking the mainsheet.

Decrease the weather yawing moment.

Very Heavy Air

Use reduced rake.

Permit maximum mast bend (to flatten the mainsail) without two-blocking the mainsheet. Allow the boom end to "float" under vang tension.

Decrease the weather yawing moment.

MAST BEND—FORE AND AFT

Significance

Determines fullness, the position of the maximum draft, and the degree to which the designed sail luff curve is matched.

Method

Streak marks on the sail at mid-height at 1-inch (or 2- or 3-inch) intervals in from the luff.

Sight the alignment of these marks with the tack and the head. Sightings can be standardized by hoisting ⅛th-inch shock cord on the headboard and, when led to the tack, noting the alignment of the shock cord with the streak marks.

Visibility

Colored tape or nail polish can be used to mark the backstay, ram, runner, or any other device used to control mast bend, and these marks can be correlated with the depth of chord of the actual mast bend. It is often not feasible to sight up the mainsail luff during a race.

Very Light Air

Use moderate bend.

Mast bend flattens the sail, thereby beneficially reducing side force and leeway, and opens the leech (which otherwise sags into an undesirably closed position).

Light Air

Use reduced bend.

If the leech will stay open, the mast bend can be reduced.

Moderate Air

Use minimum bend.

The least mast bend, the fullest sail, and the most completely closed leech are appropriate in moderate air when pointing is most effective.

Heavy to Very Heavy Air

Use increased bend.

Mast bend flattens the mainsail, reducing heeling force, leeway, and weather yawing moment, and reduces excessive jibstay sag.

MAST BEND—LATERAL

Significance

Modifies fullness and position of maximum draft in the mainsail and modifies jibstay sag.

Method

Sight the deviation of the mast from a straight line.

Plus sign may be used to record amount of tip falloff to leeward, minus sign to indicate sag of the mid-mast to leeward.

Visibility

The lower shroud turnbuckle position (or other device used to control lateral mast bend) can be marked at positions correlated with the tip falloff or sag.

Very Light Air

Use straight mast.

Lateral sag would undesirably increase fullness.

Light Air

Use increased mid-mast sag (negative bend).

As speed increases, leeway diminishes and additional power usefully increases driving force.

Moderate Air

Use maximum mid-mast sag.

Maximum speed and maximum pointing are achieved by maximum sail fullness combined with a closed leech.

Heavy Air

Use a straight mast.

Mainsail must be flattened to reduce heeling force, leeway, and weather yawing moment.

Very Heavy Air

Use tip falloff.

Mainsail must be flattened, twisted, and displaced to the least effective angle of incidence.

VANG

Significance

Controls fullness of the lower mainsail, leech closure, and jibstay sag.

Method

Observe the movement of a mark on the vang to or from a block or fairlead.

Visibility

Colored tape or nail polish can be used to designate one or more positions near the block or fairlead.

Very Light Air

No tension used.

The mainsail leech must be kept open.

Light Air

Use moderate tension.

The jibstay should be induced to sag to increase the jib's fullness, shift its draft forward, and make it more adaptable.

Moderate Air

No tension used.
The mainsail should be full and the jibstay tight.

Heavy Air (and Dirty Air and Waves)

Use moderate tension.
The mainsail should be flattened and the rig made more flexible.

Very Heavy Air

Use marked tension.
The mainsail should be very flat and twisted, the boom end floating, and the jibstay responsive.

CUNNINGHAM

Significance

Determines position of maximum draft.

Method

Sight the movement of the Cunningham eye relative to marks on the mast.

Visibility

Marks or marked tape can be placed along the mast to provide a guage of Cunningham eye movement.

Very Light to Moderate Air

No tension used.
With minimal pressure on the sail and a relatively straight mast, the position of maximum draft tends to be too far forward and, therefore, ordinarily needs no Cunningham tension.

Heavy to Very Heavy Air

Use moderate to marked tension.
In order to prevent the position of maximum draft shifting aft (with increased pressure on the sail and increased bending of the mast), the Cunningham must be progressively tensioned.

OUTHAUL

Significance
Determines fullness in the lower portion of the mainsail.

Method
Sight position of the clew relative to marks on the boom inboard of the black band.

Visibility
Marks or marked tape can be placed along the boom (inside the black band) to provide a gauge of clew movement.

Very Light Air
Use moderate tension.
The mainsail should be kept flat to reduce side force and leeway.

Light to Moderate Air
No tension used.
The mainsail should be kept full to provide maximum power.

Heavy to Very Heavy Air
Use increased to maximum tension.
The mainsail should be flattened progressively to reduce heeling, windward yawing moment, and leeway.

MAIN TRAVELER

Significance
Determines the angle of incidence and modifies the twist of the mainsail.

Method
Sight position of the traveler car (or boom) relative to marks on, or alongside, the traveler indicating distance from the centerline.

Visibility
Place marks or marked tape along or adjacent to the traveler and laterally from the centerline.

Very Light Air

Traveler car is shifted to windward with the mainsheet eased (so that the boom is over the corner of the transom) to increase driving force and reduce side force and leeway.

Light Air

Traveler car is gradually shifted toward the centerline (and mainsheet tensioned) to increase power and pointing.

Moderate Air

Traveler car is shifted to the centerline (so that the boom is on the centerline) to attain maximum pointing.

Heavy to Very Heavy Air

Traveler car is eased so that the boom is to leeward of the centerline to reduce heeling and leeway.

MAINSHEET

Significance

Determines mainsail leech tension and therefore the twist, fullness, and position of maximum draft of the mainsail and modifies jibstay sag and therefore the twist, fullness, and position of maximum draft of the jib.

Method

Sight the distance between the mainsheet blocks *or* the degrees by which the upper batten angles away from parallel to the centerline *or* variations in the flow of the upper leech telltales.

Visibility

Place marks (indelible ink) on the mainsheet or draw a dark line (or place dark tape) on the upper batten pocket (so that its position can be sighted from beneath the boom).

Determine to what extent the batten deviates from parallel to the boom. Place telltales along the upper mainsail leech.

Very Light Air

Eased to provide marked twist (to adapt to directional and velocity variations) and to flatten mainsail (to reduce side force and leeway).

Light Air

Gradually tensioned to reduce twist, increase fullness, and shift draft aft to increase power and pointing.

Moderate Air

Maximally tensioned to achieve greatest power and highest pointing.

Heavy Air

Unchanged in smooth water (while mast is bent and traveler eased) or eased in waves (while vang is tensioned) to provide twist and flexibility.

Very Heavy Air

Eased to provide twist and flexibility.

JIBSTAY SAG

Significance

Determines the position of maximum draft, fullness, and twist of the jib.

Method

Sight, from the tack, the maximum depth of chord of the jibstay sag.

Visibility

Attach a length of ⅛th-inch shock cord to the jib halyard just above the jib head and to the deck at the tack to facilitate judging the amount of sag (offset from the shock cord).

Very Light Air

Sagged as much as possible to make the jib full and shift its draft forward.

Light Air

Maximally sagged to keep the jib full and draft forward so as to increase power and speed.

Moderate Air

Straightened to flatten the luff of the jib so as to facilitate pointing.

Heavy to Very Heavy Air

Kept straight in smooth water to facilitate pointing and allowed to sag in waves to provide flexibility.

JIB LUFF TENSION

Significance

Determines the position of maximum draft of the jib.

Method

Amount of tension $(0-4+)$ indicated by the appearance of the luff (scalloping, wrinkles, smooth) or by sighting the position of a mark on the halyard relative to a reference point on the base of the mast.

Visibility

Place marks on the base of the mast and the halyard tail to indicate the amount of tension.

Very Light Air

No tension is used as the jibstay sag shifts draft forward.

Light Air

No tension is used as the jibstay sag shifts draft forward and, in smooth water, draft aft facilitates pointing.

Moderate Air

Only minimal tension is used because, although straightened jibstay shifts draft aft, draft aft facilitates pointing.

Heavy to Very Heavy Air

Increased tension is used to counteract aft shift of draft and to open leech for gust response.

JIBSHEET LEAD POSITION

Significance

Fore-and-aft position determines fullness and twist. (The same effect can be achieved by changing the sheet attachment to a clew board or, in the presence of an adjustable jib tack, by moving the entire jib up or down the jibstay.) Lateral position determines angle of incidence and twist.

Method

Sight the position of the lead on fore-and-aft or lateral tracks (or the position of attachment to the clew board or the position of the tack above the deck, if the tack is adjustable).

Visibility

Place marks or marked tape on the deck adjacent to the sheet lead tracks (or mark the clew board or the jibstay to indicate the height of the tack).

Very Light Air

Aft and outboard to twist the jib, open its leech, and decrease its angle of incidence.

Light Air

Forward and inboard to increase power and improve pointing.

Moderate Air

Maximally forward and inboard to provide maximum power and highest possible pointing.

Heavy to Very Heavy Air

Aft and outboard to reduce power and angle of incidence and to increase twist.

JIBSHEET TENSION

Significance

Determines jib leech tension and therefore the twist, fullness, and position of maximum draft of the jib.

Method

Sight the distance between the jib clew and the lead block or the position of the jib leech referrable to the centerline, the mainsail leech, or the spreader.

Visibility

Mark the jibsheet so as to determine the distance of the clew from the block or mark the spreader so as to determine the position of the jib leech and/or the deviation of the leech (at a particular height) from the centerline. A window may be placed in the mainsail to permit sighting the jib leech from the weather rail.

Very Light Air

Eased to provide maximum twist.

Light Air

Tensioned moderately to reduce twist and to increase fullness and angle of incidence so as to increase power and pointing.

Moderate Air

Tensioned to eliminate twist, maximize fullness, and shift draft aft so as to attain the greatest possible power and pointing.

Heavy Air

Tensioned to keep leech straight until gust response and/or waves require twist and flexibility.

Very Heavy Air

Eased (if necessary) to assure twist and flexibility (a length of sheet between the lead block and the clew increases flexibility).

CONTROL METHODS

PROBLEMS

To provide sail controls which are led properly, are accessible, are sufficiently powerful, are strongly secured, and are protected from fouling.

SOLUTION

Lead the Control Properly *(Fig. 10.1)*

Align the securing device with the lead block so as to eliminate friction and entanglements (check to determine the adequacy of the lead by evaluating the control line under load)

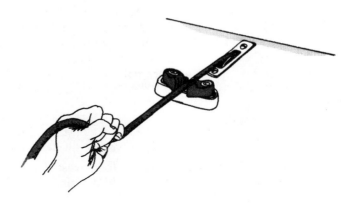

10.1 Cleat positioning. Note line lying horizontally within and opening the jaws of the cleat symmetrically.

Align the cleat (or other securing device) with the block and the expected position of the crew member so that the cleat is:
At the proper level for cleating and uncleating and so that the line when cleated lies horizontally within the cleat
Above the surrounding surface so that the line can be cleated readily without the crew member hitting his knuckles
At the proper angle so that the line opens the cleat symmetrically
Convenient to use in the most difficult of commonly encountered conditions (usually this means in heavy air)
Keep the line protected by leading it under the deck, along the topsides, along the centerboard trunk, or, if exposed, through a rigid tube

Make the Control Accessible *(Fig. 10.2)*

The accessibility of the control and its securing device should be proportionate to the frequency of its use.
"One-time controls" (main halyard, for instance) can be led to cleats in the midline (at the mast base, for instance) because they rarely need to be adjusted while racing.

"Occasional controls" (spinnaker pole topping lift and downhaul, for instance) can be led to cleats accessible only while reaching and running. However, if the crew must hike while reaching, these controls may require a swivel to permit cleating either from within the boat or from over the rail.

"Frequent controls" (sheets, vang, backstay, Cunningham, outhaul, for instance) should be led to cleats fully accessible from a hiking position or from within the boat.

Duplicate terminal controls led to each rail from either a split single lead (Cunningham or vang, for instance) or from two separate leads (jib or spinnaker sheets, for instance).

A single control led to a midline block with a swivel/cleat (mainsheet or vang, for instance), the tail of which may be taken to either side.

A continuous line connecting the tails of duplicate controls may be led through swivel/cleats on each rail for cleating to leeward (jib or spinnaker sheets, for instance).

10.2. Accessibility. Note successive multiplications of power downward at mast base, laterally to topsides, and aft to crew position.

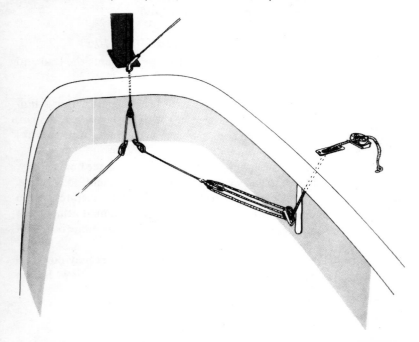

Limitations of the duplicate system:

The need to cleat (and the possibility of accidentally uncleating) the inaccessible tail on the opposite side (in order
to avoid two-blocking the accessible side) or the need
to extend the length and therefore the range of each
side to permit adequate control from one side alone.

The duplication of a vast number of blocks and line with a
consequent increase in weight (particularly when wet)
and an increased likelihood of entanglement.

Limitations of the midline swivel rig:

The need to reach to the midline to access the control line
and/or the need to take the tail to the new windward
rail with each tack (or jibe).

Limitations of the continuous line rig:

The presence of and the increased likelihood of entanglement with lines crossing the cockpit or deck.

Increased friction as the line has to be pulled through all the
blocks and leads used on the previous side.

If the control must be accessible to two (or more) different crew-
men (to use at different times), it may be mounted vertically
between the two crewman or led to a block with a swivel/cleat
in the midline or near the leeward rail.

Make the Control Sufficiently Powerful *(Fig. 10.3)*

Use a means of increasing power which complements the lead and
the accessibility of the control.

Lever: A lever multiplies power with little weight within a limited vertical span, but requires a relatively large lateral span,
has a limited range, and is likely to entangle other control
lines.

Drum: A drum multiplies power in a confined space but is heavy,
bulky, subject to disastrous overrides, and difficult to regulate.

Winch: A winch can be extremely powerful and operates within
a small space but is heavy, requires both manual attachment
and tailing, and can only be operated from within the boat (not
while hiking).

Worm gear: A worm gear apparatus can be extremely powerful
and operates within a small space but is heavy, slow, has an

extremely short range, and can only be operated from within the boat.

Ratchet block: A ratchet block is simple, compact, and light-weight but provides no additional power, merely, when statically loaded, a respite from continuous tension.

Multiple blocks in parallel: Each line leading into or out of a moving block adds a unit of power. The system is lightweight and compact (particularly if confined in a "magic box") but requires a sheave for each unit gain and the movement of a long length of line to achieve a wide range of control.

Multiple blocks in series (cascade): Each line passing through a block affixed to the tail of a line ahead multiplies the power applied. The system is lightweight, reduces the number of blocks and the length of line required, and requires the movement of only a short length of line to achieve a wide range of control, but requires, in order to attain that wide range, a long span within which to operate. For most small racing boats, this is the optimal power-enhancing method.

Permit the puller to use his legs (as well as his back and arms) to operate the control. Place the control cleat so that the crew can brace his legs horizontally (against the gunwhale, mast, centerboard trunk, barney post, etc.) or vertically (while standing above the control).

10.3. Power—parallel or cascade? Note fewer blocks but greater distance required to achieve power from cascade system.

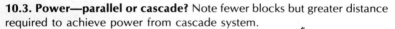

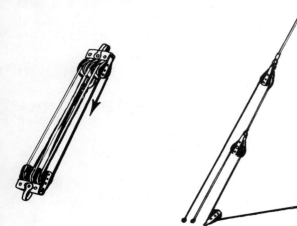

Make the Control Sufficiently Strong

Attach the control in shear rather than tension.

Align the attachment (tang, etc.) with the direction of pull of the control.

Attach the control to the sides of spars (at the neutral position relative to bend) and make round holes wherever possible.

Use bolts (machine screws) with nuts rather than screws or rivets whenever the load is great.

Use backing plates (washers or sheets of aluminum) of sufficient size so as to prevent the nut pulling through the structure.

Use lock washers (nylon or stainless steel) or peen over the bolt end or apply resin to prevent the nut from slipping.

Use blocks appropriate to the load. The first block in a multiplying cascade must be the strongest. Solid steel pins (rather than hollow tubes) and bushings (rather than ball bearings) should be used where the load is great.

Use a line which has a strength many times greater than the static load (to assure that it will tolerate the impact load), which has a covering that will not deteriorate rapidly under friction (in cam cleats, etc.), and which is large and soft enough (but only just enough—to avoid an excess weight of wet line) to be handled easily. Ease of handling is more important than a modest increase in friction.

Use lines or wires which stretch as little as possible. Wire or line with a wire or a Kevlar core should be used for segments of a control under direct load. A larger rope tail may be applied directly (for spinnaker sheets, for instance) or as the last unit in a multiple cascade series (vangs, for instance) to facilitate handling.

Avoid Entanglements

Lead control lines under the deck or by other protected routes. Use panels of Dacron to cover their course under deck or along the topsides, etc.

Keep the tails of control lines from entanglements. Use one of the following devices:

Reels: A reel rolls up a tail and prevents knots from forming on release, but is bulky and slows the release.

Shock cord: Shock cord fastened to the tail of a control line takes the tail away but can only take up a short length and reduces the accessibility of the control unless both the cleat and the fairlead are elevated (to permit getting one's hand beneath the tensioned control).

Dacron bag: A Dacron receptacle beneath the tail (which may be led by a fairlead through the deck) will confine it to a protected area.

Balls on line ends: A plastic ball on a control line tail will prevent it from escaping through a bailer.

Keep control lines from jamming when under load. Spinnaker sheets, spinnaker halyards, twings, backstay controls, etc., and any line which is led through a device such as a spinnaker pole end, or which has a spliced tail, or which is required to be released to a stopper knot, should have a metal washer (or a plastic ball) to fetch up against. This will prevent it from jamming and facilitate its subsequent release.

Glossary

TERMS

Aerodynamic Force, F_T—the force produced by air flow deviated or impeded by a sail or sails, generally proportionate to and dependent upon wind velocity, sail area, and angle of incidence

Angle of Incidence, α—the angle between the direction of apparent wind flow and the horizontal chord of the sail section, a major determinant of the aerodynamic force produced

Apparent Course Angle (Course Achieved), β—the angle between the course achieved and the direction of the apparent wind flow, equal to the heading angle plus the leeway angle

Apparent Wind, V_A —the air flow impinging upon the sails whose force and direction is resultant from the combination of true wind flow and the movement of the boat through the wind flow

Buoyancy—the vertical (upward) force consequent and equal to displacement and the weight of the yacht

Center of Buoyancy, CB—the point within the hull at which the total buoyancy force due to displacement may be presumed to act (upward)

Center of Effort, CE—the point on the sail surface (or surfaces) at which the total aerodynamic force or forces acting on the sail (or sails) may be presumed to act, (almost) always to leeward of the centerline

Center of Gravity, CG—the point within the hull at which the total weight (gravitational force) of the hull and its rig may be presumed to act (downward)

Center of Lateral Resistance, CLR—the point on the midline projection of the lateral plane of the hull and its fins at which the total hydrodynamic force acting on the hull and its fins may be presumed to act

Design Wind—The wind velocity which the maximum available righting moment will just counteract so that the boat can be sailed to windward upright (or at its optimal angle of heel) and at its maximum speed

Displacement—the weight of the volume of water displaced by and equal to the weight of the yacht

Displacement Sailing—forward motion of the yacht at slow to moderate speeds during which the hull is displacing a volume of water equal to or greater than its weight

Draft (Fullness)—The shape of the horizontal section of the sail measured by the ratio depth of chord/chord

Draft, Sectional Distribution—Variation in draft, full or flat, either side of the position of maximum draft, i.e., "flat entry," "full leading edge," etc.

Draft, Vertical Distribution—Variation in draft at various heights; when the upper sections are full aft, the leech is called "tight," when the upper sections are flat aft, the leech is called "open"

Driving Force, F_R—the element of the aerodynamic force acting forward in the direction of the course sailed

Forced Oscillation—the oscillation with its characteristic period which results when a boat is set in oscillation by wave influences

Form Drag—the drag created by the inability of air flow to deviate around an object (mast, sails, etc.) in its path without separating and forming eddies as it returns to its original path

Free Oscillation—the oscillation with its characteristic period which results when a boat is set in oscillation in calm water

Frictional Drag—the drag created by the frictional resistance of the sail surface chiefly due to its porosity

Frictional Resistance, R_F—the resistance created by the movement of the wetted surface through the water, chiefly the turbulence at the interface between water clinging to the hull and that which is flowing past, proportional to the wetted surface and the only significant resistance at low and very high (planing) speeds

Heading Angle or Pointing Angle (β-λ)—the angle between the centerline of the boat and the direction of apparent wind flow, equal to the angle of incidence plus the sheeting angle

Heeling Force, F_H—the element of the aerodynamic force acting laterally, perpendicular to the direction of the course sailed

Heeling Moment, M_H—the force couple which tends to turn the boat vertically about a horizontal axis through its CB parallel to its centerline and equal to the product of the heeling force, F_H, and the arm upon which it acts between the CE and the CLR

Hydrodynamic Force, R_T—the force produced by water flow deviated or impeded by the hull and its fins, generally proportionate to and dependent upon boat speed, fin area, and leeway angle (or angle of incidence)

Hydrodynamic Lift—the elevation of the yacht due to the vertical (buoyancy) component of the bow wave's thrust against the hull

Hydrodynamic Side Force, F_S—the element of the hydrodynamic force acting perpendicular to the course consequent to the lift created by the hull and its fins moving through the water at a speed, V_S, and a leeway angle, λ

Induced Drag—the drag induced by the production of the aerodynamic force chiefly consequent to vortex eddies about the foot and the head of the sail

Lee Helm—the angulation of the tiller (helm) to leeward, associated with the angulation of the rudder to windward, required to overcome a leeward yawing moment

Leeway Angle, λ—the angle between the centerline of the boat and the course sailed (which is required to achieve sufficient hydrodynamic side force to sail to windward)

Lift—the force produced by air or water flowing past and deviated by an arched surface which acts in the direction desired—ahead for an aerodynamic force, laterally for a hydrodynamic force

Lift: Drag Ratio—the ratio of the lift force vector to the drag force vector resultant from a force produced by a lifting surface, a measure of the efficiency of the surface

$F_R: F_H$ **Ratio**—the ratio of the aerodynamic driving force, F_R, acting in the line of the course sailed to the heeling force, F_H, acting perpendicular to the course sailed (at 90° to the driving force)

$F_S:R$ **Ratio**—the ratio of the hydrodynamic side (lift) force, F_S, acting perpendicular to the course sailed to the drag force or resistance, R, acting parallel (aft) to the course sailed

Luffing—the occurrence of a positive force directed toward the leeward sail surface when the angle of incidence becomes too low

Moment of Inertia—the resistance of the hull to oscillate and the tendency of the hull to continue oscillation once the oscillation is initiated

Parasitic Drag—the drag due to the form and frictional resistance of the hull appendages and crew

Period or Periodic Time—the time required for one oscillation

Pitching Moment, M_P—the force couple which tends to turn the boat vertically about a horizontal axis through its CB perpendicular to its centerline and equal to the product of the driving force, F_R, and the arm upon which it acts between the CE and the CB

Planing—forward motion at high speed during which hydrodynamic lift plus buoyancy exceed the weight and sinkage of the yacht and elevate it above its resting displacement level

Position of Maximum Draft—the fore and aft position of the greatest depth of chord of the horizontal sail section

"Pump Effect"—The additional driving force created when, with an abrupt increase in the angle of incidence, leeward surface flow remains attached and lift increases

Rake—the angle which the mast makes with the perpendicular to the water line

Resistance or Drag—the force directed aft along the course created by the movement of water or air about the hull, its fins, its sails, or rig (resistance usually refers to hydrodynamic resistance; drag usually refers to aerodynamic resistance)

Resonance—the reinforcement of a forced oscillation by the harmony of its period with the period of free oscillation

Reynold's Number—a value indicating the frictional resistance created by a surface of given camber and length in a flow of given viscosity and velocity

Righting Moment—The weight of crew, keel, or hull which, acting on an arm extending from the CLR, acts to equilibrate the heeling force (the reverse of the heeling moment)

Rolling Moment, M_R—the force couple which tends to turn the boat vertically about a horizontal axis through its CB parallel to its centerline and equal to the product of the rolling force and the arm upon which it acts between the CE or CLR (or other point of action) and the CB

Semiplaning—forward motion of the yacht at moderately high speeds during which hydrodynamic lift is adding to buoyancy in elevating the yacht

Sheeting Angle (Angle of Trim), δ—the angle between the horizontal chord of the sail section and the centerline of the yacht

Sinkage—the depression of the yacht due to the alterations in displacement and buoyancy consequent to wave making

Slope Drag—the horizontal (forward) acting component of the forces of gravity acting perpendicular to the general water level and buoyancy acting perpendicular to the wave face, resulting in forward motion of the yacht down the wave face

Stalling—the occurrence of separated, turbulent leeward surface flow, when the angle of incidence becomes so great that flow is unable to deviate sufficiently to remain attached

Surfing—the utilization of slope drag to achieve semiplaning speeds and to acquire the benefits of hydrodynamic lift

Twist—the variation in the direction of the chords of the horizontal sail sections at different heights associated with a decreasing angle of incidence with height

Unbalanced Arm—the distance between the directions of actions of two forces which determine a turning moment

Wave-making Resistance, R_W—the resistance created by the production of waves by the hull as it is driven through the water, the major resistance at moderate to high speeds, and the limitation on displacement sailing speed

Weather Helm—the angulation of the tiller (helm) to weather associated with the angulation of the rudder to leeward required to overcome a windward yawing moment

Wetted Surface—the area of the hull and fin surface which is immersed in the water and determines the frictional resistance

Yawing Moment, M_y—the force couple which tends to turn the boat horizontally about a vertical axis through its CLR and equal to the product of the lateral element of the heeling force, F_{lat}, and the unbalanced arm between the direction of actions of F_T and R_T (may be a windward or leeward yawing moment—tending to turn the bow to windward or leeward)

Charts

CHART 1. Summary: Gears and Controls

Gear	Head-ing	Mast Bend	Main-sheet Twist	Vang	Outhaul	Cunning-ham	Boom Traveler Car	Jibstay Sag	Jibsheet	Jib Luff	Jib Lead
Go Gear	Down	Decreased	Twist	Tension	Ease	Ease	Inboard	Increased	Twist	Tension	Inboard
Low Leeway Gear	Down	Increased	Twist (SL)	Tension	Tension	Tension	Outboard	Moderate	Twist (SL)	Tension	Outboard
Pointing Gear	Up	Increased	Tension	Ease	Tension	Ease	Inboard	Decreased	Tension	Ease	Inboard
Starting Gear	Up	Decreased → Increased	Twist → Closed	—	Ease → Tension	No Change → Tension	Inboard → No Change	Increased → Decreased	Twist → Closed	Tension → No Change	Inboard → No Change
Wave Control	Down	Decreased	Twist	Tension	Ease	Ease	Inboard	Increased	Twist	Tension	Inboard
Gust Control	Up	Increased	Twist	Tension	Tension	Tension	Outboard	Moderate	Twist	Tension	Outboard
Heavy Air Control	Down	Increased	Twist	Tension	Tension	Tension	Outboard	Increased (Vang)	Twist	Tension	Outboard (slightly)

CHART 2. *Sail Selection Chart*

	Main	Jib	Mast Bend	Vang	Twist	Jibstay Sag
Very Light Air 1–3 Knots	Minimal luff curve Tight-leeched main	Minimal luff curve Full jib	3"	0	3+	2"
Light Air 4–6 Knots	"	"	2"	2+	2+	3"
Moderate Air 7–14 Knots	"	"	3"	0	0	1"
Moderate Air 7–14 Knots Waves	"	Big luff curve Flat jib	3"	2+	2+	3"
Heavy Air 15–25 Knots	Big luff curve Open-leeched main	"	6"–8"	3+	2+	3"
Very Heavy Air 25+ Knots	"	"	10"	4+	4+	4"+

CHART 3A. Blank Trim Chart

Wind	Date Circumstance	Mast			Mainsail:					Boom	Jib:						
		Rake	Bend	Sag Lateral	Sheet	Battens	Vang	Outhaul	Cunn.	Traveler Car	Sheet	Twist	Sag	Luff	Tack	Lead Fore +Aft	Lead Lateral
Smooth			+½"	-½"	+1"	-2°	-	-	+	-3"	+	+	-	-	+	Aft	Out
Waves			-½"	+½"	-1"	+2°	+	+	-	TWIST +3"	-	-	+	+	-	Fwd	In
1-2																	
2-3																	
3-4																	
2-IN 4-5																	
5-6																	
6-7																	
2-Deck 7-8																	

8–9												
9–10												
10–11												
2-Hike 11–12												
13–14												
15–16												
17–18												
19–20												
21–22												
23–24												
25–30												
30+												

CHART 3B. Light Air Mainsail and Jib.

Wind	Date Circum- stance	Mast			Mainsail:					Boom	Jib:						
		Rake	Bend	Sag Lat- eral	Sheet	Bat- tens	Vang	Out- haul	Cunn.	Trav- eler Car	Sheet	Twist	Sag	Luff	Tack	Lead Fore +Aft	Lead Lat-
Smooth			+½"	-½"	+1"	-2°	-	-	+	-3"	+	+	-	-	+	Aft	Out
Waves			-½"	+½"	-1"	+2°	+	+	-	TWIST +3"	-	-	+	+	-	Fwd	In
1-2					24"		0	-2"	0	+15"	8"	4+		EASY		AFT	16"
2-3		25½"	3"	0	15"	5°mm	0	-2"	0	-8"	6"	3+			2"↑		15"
3-4				-7¾"	12"	4°mm	0	-2"	0							2	14"
2-IN 4-5	SSA SPRING 83	25½"	2"		8"	2°mm	1+	-2"	0	+3"	2½"	2+	6"	EASY	2	2	12"
5-6			2"	-1¾"	5"	2°mm	2+	-2"	0	+3"	2½"	2+			1½"	2	11½"
6-7			2"	-1¾"			0										
2-Deck 7-8			2"														

Range	Notes												WRIN-KLES				
8-9		25½"	2"	-1¾"	3"	0°	0	-3"	0	+3"	2"	0	2"			2	1½"
9-10		25½"	1½"	-1"	2"	0°	0	-3"	0	+3"	2"	0	2"		1"	2	1½"
10-11	WINTER MAR 20		1½"	-1"	1"	0°	0	-3"	0	+3"	2"	0	2"		1"	2	1½"
2-Hike 11-12	ST. PETE THURS.	24½"	"	-1"	2 BLOCK	1°	0	-2"	0	+3"	1½"	0	2½"	1+	½"	2	1½"
13-14	WINTER JAN 30		3½"		2 BLOCK	1°	1+	-1"	1+	0		0	3"	1+	0"	2	12"
15-16	SSA SPRING 83 SERIES		5"	-1"	2 BLOCK	2°	2+	-½"	2+	0-3"	1"	1+	4"	2+		2	14"
17-18		23½"		0												2	16"
19-20			7"	0	FLOAT	5°	4+	0	3+	-6"-18"		3+		2+	0"	AFT	16"
21-22				+1"													
23-24																	
25-30																	
30+																	

CHART 3C. Heavy Air Mainsail and Jib.

Wind	Date Circum-stance	Mast Rake	Mast Bend	Mast Sag Lateral	Mainsail: Sheet	Mainsail: Battens	Mainsail: Vang	Mainsail: Outhaul	Mainsail: Cunn.	Boom: Traveler Car	Jib: Sheet	Jib: Twist	Jib: Sag	Jib: Luff	Jib: Tack	Jib: Lead Fore +Aft	Jib: Lead Lat-
Smooth			+½"	-½"	+1"	-2°	-	-	+	-3"	+	+	-	-	+	Aft	Out
Waves			-½"	+½"	-1"	+2°	+	+	-	TWIST +3"	-	-	+	+	-	Fwd	In
1-2																	
2-3																	
3-4																	
2-IN 4-5																	
5-6																	
6-7	ST. PETE TEST	Ð5½"	5½"		0-3"	1°ω	+	-2"	0	+3"	3"	0	3" EASY	½	½↑	2	1½"
2-Deck 7-8																	

8-9													
9-10	Mc DIAMOND												
10-11	25½"	5"	0	2"w		+3"		3°	3" EASY	1½"	2		
2-Hike 11-12	25½"	6"	0	3°		+3"	2"	5°	3½" EASY	1½"	2	12½"
13-14		8"	+½"	2"	4°	3+	0	1½"	8°	4"	1"	2	
15-16													
17-18	WINTER MAR. 13	9"	+1"	3"	5°	3+	-3"	1½"	10°	5"	½	AFT	14"
19-20		9"		4"	10°	4+	-6"			6"			
21-22	ST. PETE WED	25½"	9½"	4"		4+	-6"	1"	10°	6"	3+	0	3	15"
23-24	SPRING DARLING BOM. '83	10"	+2"		10°	FLOAT 4+	0-6"						
25-30	RUSH CREEK SPRING '83	23"	10"	+3"	5"	10°	FLOAT 4+	12"	2"	10°	6"	4+	0	4	16"
30+													